I0473903

U.S. Department of Justice
Office of Justice Programs
810 Seventh Street N.W.
Washington, DC 20531

Janet Reno
Attorney General

Daniel Marcus
Acting Associate Attorney General

Mary Lou Leary
Acting Assistant Attorney General

Julie E. Samuels
Acting Director, National Institute of Justice

Office of Justice Programs
World Wide Web Site
http://www.ojp.usdoj.gov

National Institute of Justice
World Wide Web Site
http://www.ojp.usdoj.gov/nij

Full Report of the Prevalence, Incidence, and Consequences of Violence Against Women

Patricia Tjaden
Nancy Thoennes

**Findings From the National
Violence Against Women Survey**

November 2000
NCJ 183781

CENTERS FOR DISEASE CONTROL
AND PREVENTION

Julie E. Samuels
Acting Director, National Institute of Justice

Stephen B. Thacker
Acting Director, National Center for Injury Prevention and Control

This research was sponsored under award number 93–IJ–CX–0012 by the National Institute of Justice, Office of Justice Programs, U.S. Department of Justice, and the Centers for Disease Control and Prevention. Findings and conclusions of the research presented here are those of the authors and do not necessarily reflect the official position or policies of the U.S. Department of Justice.

The National Institute of Justice is a component of the Office of Justice Programs, which also includes the Bureau of Justice Assistance, the Bureau of Justice Statistics, the Office of Juvenile Justice and Delinquency Prevention, and the Office for Victims of Crime.

Executive Summary

Key Issues

Research on violence against women has exploded in the past 20 years, particularly in the areas of intimate partner violence and sexual assault. Despite this outpouring of research, many gaps exist in our understanding of violence against women. For instance, reliable information on minority women's experiences with violence is still lacking. Few empirical data exist on the relationship between different forms of violence against women, such as victimization in childhood and subsequent victimization. Finally, empirical data on the consequences of violence against women, including their injury rates and use of medical services, are lacking.

To further understanding of violence against women, the National Institute of Justice and the Centers for Disease Control and Prevention jointly sponsored, through a grant to the Center for Policy Research, a national survey that was conducted from November 1995 to May 1996. The National Violence Against Women (NVAW) Survey sampled both women and men and thus provides comparable data on women's and men's experiences with violent victimization.

Respondents to the survey were asked about:

- Physical assault they experienced as children by adult caretakers.

- Physical assault they experienced as adults by any type of assailant.

- Forcible rape and stalking they experienced at any time in their life by any type of perpetrator.

Respondents who disclosed that they had been victimized were asked detailed questions about the characteristics and consequences of their victimization, including injuries they sustained and their use of medical services.

This NIJ Research Report presents findings from the NVAW Survey on the prevalence and incidence of rape, physical assault, and stalking; the rate of injury among rape and physical assault victims; and injured victims' use of medical services. The data show that violence is more widespread and injurious to women's and men's health than previously thought—an important finding for legislators, policymakers, intervention planners, and researchers as well as the public health and criminal justice communities.

Key Findings

Analysis of survey data on the prevalence, incidence, and consequences of violence against women produced the following results:

- Physical assault is widespread among adults in the United States: 51.9 percent of surveyed women and 66.4 percent of surveyed men said they were physically assaulted as a child by an adult caretaker and/or as an adult by any type of attacker. An estimated 1.9 million women and 3.2 million men are physically assaulted annually in the United States.

- Many American women are raped at an early age: Of the 17.6 percent of all women surveyed who said they had been the victim of a completed or attempted rape at some time in their life, 21.6 percent were younger than age 12 when they were first raped, and 32.4 percent were ages 12 to 17. Thus, more than half (54 percent) of the female rape victims identified by the survey were younger than age 18 when they experienced their first attempted or completed rape.

- Stalking is more prevalent than previously thought: 8.1 percent of surveyed women and 2.2 percent of surveyed men reported being stalked at some time in their life; 1.0 percent of women surveyed and 0.4 percent of men surveyed reported being stalked in the 12 months preceding the survey. Approximately 1 million women and 371,000 men are stalked annually in the United States.

- American Indian/Alaska Native women and men report more violent victimization than do women and men of other racial backgrounds: American Indian/Alaska Native women were significantly more likely than white women, African-American women, or mixed-race women to report they were raped. They also were significantly more likely than white women or African-American women to report they were stalked. American Indian/Alaska Native men were significantly more likely than Asian men to report they were physically assaulted.

- Rape prevalence varies between Hispanic and non-Hispanic women: Hispanic women were significantly less likely than non-Hispanic women to report they were raped at some time in their life.

- There is a relationship between victimization as a minor and subsequent victimization: Women who reported they were raped before age 18 were twice as likely to report being raped as an adult. Women who reported they were physically assaulted as a child by an adult caretaker were twice as likely to report being physically assaulted as an adult. Women who reported they were stalked before age 18 were seven times more likely to report being stalked as an adult.

- Women experience more intimate partner violence than do men: 22.1 percent of surveyed women, compared with 7.4 percent of surveyed men, reported they were physically assaulted by a current or former spouse, cohabiting partner, boyfriend or girlfriend, or date in their lifetime; 1.3 percent of surveyed women and 0.9 percent of surveyed men reported experiencing such violence in the previous 12 months. Approximately 1.3 million women and 835,000 men are physically assaulted by an intimate partner annually in the United States.

- Violence against women is primarily intimate partner violence: 64.0 percent of the women who reported being raped, physically assaulted, and/or stalked since age 18 were victimized by a current or former husband, cohabiting partner, boyfriend, or date. In comparison, only 16.2 percent of the men who reported being raped and/or physically assaulted since age 18 were victimized by such a perpetrator.

- Women are significantly more likely than men to be injured during an assault: 31.5 percent of female rape victims, compared with 16.1 percent of male rape victims, reported being injured during their most recent rape; 39.0 percent of female physical assault victims, compared with 24.8 percent of male physical assault victims, reported being injured during their most recent physical assault.

- The risk of injury increases among female rape and physical assault victims when their assailant is a current or former intimate: Women who were raped or physically assaulted by a current or former spouse, cohabiting partner, boyfriend, or date were significantly more likely than women who were raped or physically assaulted by other types of perpetrators to report being injured during their most recent rape or physical assault.

- Approximately one-third of injured female rape and physical assault victims receive medical treatment: 35.6 percent of the women injured during their most recent rape and 30.2 percent of the women injured during their most recent physical assault received medical treatment.

Policy Implications

Information generated by the NVAW Survey validates opinions held by professionals in the field about the pervasiveness and injurious consequences of violence against women. This study's findings on the frequency with which women are victimized by intimate partners confirms previous reports that violence against women is primarily intimate partner violence. The study makes it clear that violence against women, particularly intimate partner violence, should be classified as a major public health and criminal justice concern in the United States. The large number of rape, physical assault, and stalking victimizations committed against women each year and the early age at which violence starts for many women strongly suggest that violence against women is endemic. Because most victimizations are perpetrated against women by current and former intimates and because women are more likely to be injured if their assailant is a current or former intimate, violence prevention strategies for women that focus on how they can protect themselves from intimate partners are needed. Injury and medical utilization data provide compelling evidence of the physical and social costs associated with violence against women. The findings suggest that future researchers should pay greater attention to demographic, social, and environmental factors that may account for variations in victimization rates among women of different racial and ethnic backgrounds and to the link between victimization they experience as a minor and subsequent victimization.

Other Publications From the National Violence Against Women Survey

Other NIJ publications provide additional information on the National Violence Against Women Survey:

- *Stalking in America: Findings From the National Violence Against Women Survey,* Research in Brief, by Patricia Tjaden and Nancy Thoennes, Washington, DC: U.S. Department of Justice, National Institute of Justice, 1998, NCJ 169592. This document provides detailed information from the survey on women's and men's experiences with stalking.

- *Prevalence, Incidence, and Consequences of Violence Against Women: Findings From the National Violence Against Women Survey,* Research in Brief, by Patricia Tjaden and Nancy Thoennes, Washington, DC: U.S. Department of Justice, National Institute of Justice, 1998, NCJ 172837. This document summarizes the findings presented in this Research Report.

- *Extent, Nature, and Consequences of Intimate Partner Violence: Findings From the National Violence Against Women Survey,* Research Report, by Patricia Tjaden and Nancy Thoennes, Washington, DC: U.S. Department of Justice, National Institute of Justice, 2000, NCJ 181867. This document provides detailed information from the survey on women's and men's experiences with intimate partner violence.

To obtain copies of these publications, visit NIJ's Web site at: *http://www.ojp.usdoj.gov/nij,* or contact the National Criminal Justice Reference Service, P.O. Box 6000, Rockville, MD 20849–6000; 800–851–3420 or 301–519–5500; or send an e-mail message to *askncjrs@ncjrs.org.*

The following journal articles have been or will be published about the NVAW Survey:

- Patricia Tjaden and Nancy Thoennes, "Co-Worker Violence and Gender: Findings From the National Violence Against Women Survey," *American Journal of Preventive Medicine,* Special Edition on Workplace Violence, Vol. 20, Issue 1 (forthcoming 2001).

- Patricia Tjaden and Nancy Thoennes, "Effects of Interviewer Gender on Men's Responses to a Telephone Survey on Violent Victimization," *Journal of Quantitative Criminology* (forthcoming 2001).

- Patricia Tjaden, Nancy Thoennes, and Christine Allison, "Comparing Stalking Victimization from Legal and Victim Perspectives," *Violence and Victims,* Vol. 15, No. 1 (2000): 1–16.

- Patricia Tjaden and Nancy Thoennes, "Prevalence and Incidence of Violence Against Women: Findings from the National Violence Against Women Survey," *The Criminologist,* Vol. 24, No. 3, (May/June 1999): 1, 4, 13–14.

- Patricia Tjaden and Nancy Thoennes, "Prevalence and Consequences of Male-to-Female and Female-to-Male Partner Violence as Measured by the National Violence Against Women Survey," *Violence Against Women,* Vol. 6, No. 2 (February 2000): 142–161.

- Patricia Tjaden, Nancy Thoennes, Christine Allison, "Comparing Violence Over the Lifespan in Samples of Same-Sex and Opposite-Sex Cohabitants," *Violence and Victims,* Vol. 14, No. 4 (1999): 413–425.

National Violence Against Women Survey Methodology Report by Patricia Tjaden, Steve Leadbetter, John Boyle, and Robert A. Bardwell provides a more detailed account of the survey methods. This document is under review at the Centers for Disease Control and Prevention (CDC).

To learn about CDC prevention activities related to family violence and intimate partner violence, visit CDC's National Center for Injury Prevention and Control Web site at *http://www.cdc.gov/ncipc/dvp/fivpt.*

Acknowledgments

The National Violence Against Women Survey was supported by a grant to the Center for Policy Research from the U.S. Department of Justice's National Institute of Justice and the U.S. Department of Health and Human Service's Centers for Disease Control and Prevention. The authors thank Lois Mock at the National Institute of Justice and Linda Saltzman at the Centers for Disease Control and Prevention for their advice and support in completing this project. The authors also thank Holly Johnson at Statistics Canada and Kirk Williams at the University of Colorado's Center for the Study and Prevention of Violence for their help with the survey design. Finally, the authors thank Marcie-jo Kresnow, mathematical statistician at the Centers for Disease Control and Prevention, for her thorough review and helpful comments on drafts of the report.

Contents

Exhibits

1. Survey Background

Violence against women first came to be viewed as a serious social problem in the early 1970s, in part because of the re-emergence of the women's movement.[1] In unprecedented numbers, scholars trained in such diverse disciplines as philosophy, literature, law, and sociology examined violence against women in the context of a feminist ideology.[2] Despite the resulting outpouring of research on violence against women, particularly in the areas of rape and intimate partner violence, many gaps remain.[3]

Until now, for instance, empirical data on the relationship between childhood victimization and subsequent victimization were lacking. Reliable information on minority women's experiences with violence also was limited. In addition, reliable data on the consequences of violence against women, including their injury rates and use of medical services, were limited.[4]

To further an understanding of violence against women, the Centers for Disease Control and Prevention (CDC) and the National Institute of Justice (NIJ) jointly sponsored—through a grant to the Center for Policy Research—a national telephone survey on women's experiences with violence, conducted from November 1995 to May 1996. The National Violence Against Women (NVAW) Survey consisted of interviews with both women and men, thus providing comparable data on women's and men's experiences with violent victimization.

NVAW Survey respondents were queried about a wide range of topics, including:

- Physical assault they experienced as children by adult caretakers.

- Physical assault they experienced as adults by any type of assailant.

Unique Features of the National Violence Against Women Survey

Several features of the NVAW Survey set it apart from other victimization surveys:

- State-of-the-art techniques protected the confidentiality of the information being gathered and minimized the potential for retraumatizing victims of violence and jeopardizing the safety of respondents. In addition to lessening the possibility that respondents would be harmed as a result of their participation in the survey, these techniques were likely to have improved the quality of the information being gathered.

- Information about both the prevalence (lifetime and annual) and incidence of violence was gathered. Victimization estimates from the NVAW Survey can be compared with victimization estimates from many other surveys.

- Multiple, behaviorally specific questions (rather than single, direct questions) were used to screen respondents for rape, physical assault, and stalking victimization. These questions were designed to leave little doubt in the respondent's mind as to the type of information being sought.

- Detailed information about the characteristics and consequences of victimization for each type of perpetrator identified by the respondent was gathered. Although this approach created a very complicated dataset, it also created the opportunity to track victimizations by the same perpetrator (e.g., the victim's first former husband).

- Forcible rape and stalking they experienced at any time in their life by any type of perpetrator.

Respondents who disclosed that they had been victimized were asked detailed questions about the characteristics and consequences of their victimization, including injuries they sustained and their use of medical services.

This NIJ Research Report summarizes the survey's findings on the prevalence and incidence of rape, physical assault, and stalking; the prevalence of rape, physical assault, and stalking among women and men of different racial backgrounds and between women and men of Hispanic and non-Hispanic origin; the prevalence of male-to-female and female-to-male intimate partner violence; the relationship between victimization as a minor and subsequent victimization; the rate of injury among rape and physical assault victims; and injured victims' use of medical services.

A condensed version of this report has been previously published and is available through the National Institute of Justice's Research in Brief series. (See "Other Publications From the National Violence Against Women Survey" in the Executive Summary.)

Notes

1. Kennedy, L.W., in Foreword to *Dangerous Domains: Violence Against Women in Canada* by Holly Johnson, Scarborough, Ontario: International Thomas Publishing, 1996.

2. Wilson, C.F., *Violence Against Women: An Annotated Bibliography,* Boston: G.K. Hall & Co., 1981.

3. National Research Council, *Understanding Violence Against Women,* Washington, DC: National Academy Press, 1996: 40–44.

4. Ibid.

2. Survey Methods

The National Violence Against Women (NVAW) Survey was conducted from November 1995 to May 1996 by interviewers at Schulman, Ronca, Bucuvalas, Inc. (SRBI) under the direction of John Boyle.[1] The authors of this report designed the survey, edited the data, and conducted the analysis.

Respondents to the survey were queried about:

- Their level of concern about their personal safety.

- Their marital and cohabiting relationship history.

- Their sociodemographic characteristics.

- Their use of drugs and alcohol.

- Their general state of physical and mental health.

- Their current partner's sociodemographic characteristics.

- Emotional abuse by current and former spouses and cohabiting partners.

- Physical assault by adult caretakers experienced as children.

- Physical assault by other adults experienced as adults.

- Forcible rape and stalking by any type of perpetrator experienced at any time in their life.

Respondents who disclosed victimization were asked detailed questions about the characteristics and consequences of their victimization, including the victim-perpetrator relationship; the frequency and duration of the violence; the extent and nature of injuries they sustained; their use of medical, mental health, and criminal justice services; and their time lost from routine activities.

Generating the Sample

The NVAW Survey sample was drawn by random-digit dialing (RDD) from households with a telephone in the 50 States and the District of Columbia. The sample was administered by U.S. Census region. Within each region, a simple random sample of working residential "hundred banks" of phone numbers was drawn. (A hundred bank is the first 8 digits of any 10-digit telephone number; e.g., 301–608–38XX). A randomly generated 2-digit number was appended to each randomly sampled hundred bank to produce the full 10-digit, random-digit number. Separate banks of numbers were generated for male and female respondents. These random-digit numbers were called by SRBI interviewers from their central telephone facility in New York City, where nonworking and nonresidential numbers (e.g., businesses, institutions, churches, halfway houses, and dormitories) were screened out. Once a residential household was reached, eligible adults (i.e., women and men age 18 and older) in each household were identified. In households with more than one eligible adult, the adult with the most recent birthday was selected as the designated respondent.

Conducting the Interviews

A total of 8,000 women and 8,005 men age 18 and older were interviewed using a computer-assisted telephone interviewing (CATI) system. (Five completed interviews with men were subsequently eliminated from the sample during data editing due to an excessive amount of missing and inconsistent data.) Interviews with female respondents were conducted from November 1995 to May 1996, and interviews with male respondents were conducted from February to May 1996.

Household Participation Rate

The participation rate for the NVAW Survey was calculated by dividing the number of completed interviews (including those that were screened out because they were ineligible) by the total number of completed interviews, screened-out interviews, refusals, and terminated interviews.* In the female survey, interviews were deemed ineligible if there was no adult female in the household. Similarly, in the male survey, interviews were deemed ineligible if there was no adult male in the household. Note that the inclusion of screened-out (ineligible) interviews in the numerator and denominator of the formula is mathematically equivalent to adjusting the number of refusals prior to screening by the estimated rate of noneligibility. This is necessary because it is unknown how many refusals prior to screening would have resulted in ineligible interviews. Using this formula, the participation rate was 72 percent for female respondents [(8,000 + 4,829) ÷ (8,000 + 4,829 + 4,608 + 351) = 0.72] and 69 percent for male respondents [(8,005 + 8,828) ÷ (8,005 + 8,828 + 7,552 + 62) = 0.69].

---

* The formula used to calculate the participation rate is based on a study conducted by the Council for Marketing and Opinion Research; see "Refusal Rates and Industry Image Survey: Summary of Results," Council of Applied Survey Research Organizations, 3 Upper Devon, Port Jefferson, NY, 11777.

Only female interviewers surveyed female respondents. To test for possible interviewer gender effects when interviewing males, a split sample approach was used with male respondents in which half of the interviews were conducted by male interviewers and half by female interviewers.[2] A Spanish-language translation of the survey was administered by bilingual interviewers for Spanish-speaking respondents.

Completed interviews averaged 25 minutes with female respondents and 26 minutes with male respondents. Spanish-language interviews were slightly longer, averaging 32 minutes with female respondents and 33 minutes with male respondents.

Survey Screening Questions

Rape

Rape was defined as an event that occurred without the victim's consent, that involved the use or threat of force to penetrate the victim's vagina or anus by penis, tongue, fingers, or object, or the victim's mouth by penis. The definition included both attempted and completed rape. The survey used questions adapted from the National Women's Study[3] to screen respondents for rape victimization:

- [Female respondents only] *Has a man or boy ever made you have sex by using force or threatening to harm you or someone close to you? Just so there is no mistake, by sex we mean putting a penis in your vagina.*

- *Has anyone, male or female, ever made you have oral sex by using force or threat of force? Just so there is no mistake, by oral sex we mean that a man or boy put his penis in your mouth or someone, male or female, penetrated your vagina or anus with their mouth.*

- *Has anyone ever made you have anal sex by using force or threat of harm? Just so there is no mistake, by anal sex we mean that a man or boy put his penis in your anus.*

- *Has anyone, male or female, ever put fingers or objects in your vagina or anus against your will or by using force or threats?*

- *Has anyone, male or female, ever **attempted** to make you have vaginal, oral, or anal sex against your will but intercourse or penetration did not occur?*

Physical assault

Physical assault was defined as behaviors that threaten, attempt, or actually inflict physical harm. This definition is similar to the description of physical assault used in the National Family Violence Survey[4] and the Violence Against Women in Canada survey[5] and is roughly equivalent to what is legally referred to as simple and aggravated assault. A modified version of the Conflict Tactics Scale[6] (CTS) was used to screen respondents for physical assault they experienced as a child at the hands of an adult caretaker and physical assault they experienced as an adult at the hands of another adult:

- *[Physical assault as a child] Aside from any incidents already mentioned, when you were a child, did any parent, stepparent, or guardian ever . . .*

- *[Physical assault as an adult] Not counting any incidents you have already mentioned, after you became an adult, did any other adult, male or female, ever . . .*

  - *Throw something at you that could hurt?*

  - *Push, grab, or shove you?*

  - *Pull your hair?*

  - *Slap or hit you?*

  - *Kick or bite you?*

  - *Choke or attempt to drown you?*

  - *Hit you with some object?*

  - *Beat you up?*

  - *Threaten you with a gun?*

  - *Threaten you with a knife or other weapon?*

  - *Use a gun on you?*

  - *Use a knife or other weapon on you?*

It should be noted that the decision to use behaviorally specific acts contained in the CTS to screen respondents for physical assault victimization was intended to circumvent the imprecision and subjectivity possible when respondents are asked about such abstractions as "assault." Because this approach does not take into account the context in which these acts are committed, it is possible some *yes* responses given by respondents to questions contained in the CTS may have involved incidents that respondents did not consider to be assaultive. To mitigate the potential for exaggerating the prevalence and incidence of physical assaults that can occur when a behaviorally objective instrument such as the CTS is used, the NVAW Survey introduced questions about physical assault by adult caretakers sustained in childhood with the following statement: *Now, I'm going to ask you some questions about* **violence** *you may have experienced as a child.* This introductory statement was intended to alert respondents to the fact the survey solicited information about acts of malicious and purposeful harm that may have been perpetrated by adult caretakers against them as children, rather than harmless or even beneficial acts. No such statement was used to introduce questions about physical assault experienced as an adult.

Stalking

The definition of stalking used in the NVAW Survey closely resembles the definition of stalking used in the model antistalking code for States developed by the National Institute of Justice.[7] The survey defines stalking as a course of conduct directed at a specific person that involves repeated visual or physical proximity; nonconsensual communication; verbal, written, or implied threats; or a combination thereof that would cause fear in a reasonable person (with *repeated* meaning on two or more occasions). As in the model antistalking code, the definition of stalking used in the NVAW Survey does not require stalkers to make a credible threat of violence against victims, but it does require victims to feel a high level of fear ("fear of bodily harm").

The survey used the following questions to screen for stalking victimization:

- *Not including bill collectors, telephone solicitors, or other salespeople, has anyone, male or female, ever . . .*

  — *Followed or spied on you?*

  — *Sent you unsolicited letters or written correspondence?*

  — *Made unsolicited phone calls to you?*

  — *Stood outside your home, school, or workplace?*

  — *Showed up at places you were even though he or she had no business being there?*

  — *Left unwanted items for you to find?*

  — *Tried to communicate in other ways against your will?*

  — *Vandalized your property or destroyed something you loved?*

Respondents who answered *yes* to one or more of these questions were asked whether anyone had ever done any of these things to them on more than one occasion and whether they felt frightened or feared bodily harm as a result of these behaviors. Only respondents who reported being victimized *on more than one occasion,* and who were *very frightened or feared bodily harm* were counted as stalking victims.

In addition to being asked behaviorally specific questions about whether they had ever experienced any number of acts associated with stalking, respondents were asked direct questions about their stalking experiences, including whether they had ever been stalked by anyone, and if so, how many different persons had stalked them; whether that person was a spouse, ex-spouse, live-in partner, boyfriend, girlfriend, date, someone else they knew, or a stranger; and what the person did that they considered to be stalking. These questions, which were asked during the introductory stage of the interview, were designed to generate information about the prevalence and characteristics of stalking from the victim's perspective rather than a legal perspective. A comparison of victim and legal

perspectives on stalking using data from the NVAW Survey is summarized in an article written by the authors.[8]

Victim-perpetrator relationship

Respondents who responded affirmatively to the behaviorally specific rape, physical assault, or stalking screening questions were asked whether their perpetrator was a current or former spouse, a male live-in partner, a female live-in partner, a relative, someone else they knew, or a stranger. Respondents disclosing violence by a former spouse or cohabiting partner were asked to specify which spouse/partner victimized them (e.g., first former husband or current male live-in partner). Respondents disclosing violence by a relative were asked to specify which relative victimized them (e.g., father, brother, or uncle). Finally, respondents disclosing violence by someone else they knew were asked to specify the relationship this person had with them (e.g., date, boyfriend, girlfriend, boss, teacher, or neighbor). Perpetrators who were current or former spouses, cohabiting partners, boyfriends/girlfriends, and dates were classified as intimate partners.

Characteristics and consequences of violence

To generate information on the characteristics and consequences of violence, respondents disclosing victimization were asked detailed questions about the *most recent* violent incident they had experienced at the hands of each perpetrator they identified. Included were questions about the location of the incident; the victim's and perpetrator's use of drugs and alcohol at the time of the incident; the perpetrator's use of weapons and threats; the victim's fear of bodily harm or death; injuries sustained by the victim; the victim's use of medical, mental health, and justice system services; and the victim's time lost from work, school, household chores, recreational activities, and volunteer endeavors.

Data Analysis

Data were analyzed using SPSS Base 7.0 for Windows software. Measures of association (e.g.,

Exhibit 1. Estimated Standard Errors Multiplied by the Z-Score (1.96) for a 95-Percent Confidence Level by Sample or Subsample Size					
Size of Sample or Subsample	Percentage of the Sample or Subsample Giving a Certain Response or Displaying a Certain Characteristic for Percentages Exactly or Approximately Equal to:				
	10 or 90	20 or 80	30 or 70	40 or 60	50/50
16,000	0.5	0.6	0.7	0.8	0.8
12,000	0.6	0.7	0.8	0.9	0.9
8,000	0.7	0.9	1.0	1.1	1.1
4,000	0.9	1.2	1.4	1.5	1.5
3,000	1.1	1.4	1.6	1.8	1.8
2,000	1.3	1.8	2.0	2.1	2.2
1,500	1.5	2.0	2.3	2.5	2.5
1,300	1.6	2.2	2.5	2.7	2.7
1,200	1.7	2.3	2.6	2.8	2.8
1,100	1.8	2.4	2.7	2.9	3.0
1,000	1.9	2.5	2.8	3.0	3.1
900	2.0	2.6	3.0	3.2	3.3
800	2.1	2.8	3.2	3.4	3.5
700	2.2	3.0	3.4	3.6	3.7
600	2.4	3.2	3.7	3.9	4.0
500	2.6	3.5	4.0	4.3	4.4
400	2.9	3.9	4.5	4.8	4.9
300	3.4	4.5	5.2	5.6	5.7
200	4.2	5.6	6.4	6.8	6.9
150	4.8	6.4	7.4	7.9	8.0
100	5.9	7.9	9.0	9.7	9.8
75	6.8	9.1	10.4	11.2	11.4
50	8.4	11.2	12.8	13.7	14.0

Lambda) were calculated between nominal-level independent and dependent variables, and the chi-square statistic and Tukey's B were used to test for statistically significant differences between groups (e.g., men and women) and among groups (e.g., whites, African-Americans, Asians/Pacific Islanders, American Indians/Alaska Natives, and persons of mixed race). When the analysis included interval level dependent variables (e.g., number of victimizations), analysis of variance was employed to test for statistically significant differences between groups. Only differences with a p-value of ≤ 0.05 were considered statistically significant and are discussed in this report.

Any estimates based on fewer than five responses were deemed unreliable and, therefore, were not tested for statistically significant differences between or among groups and not presented in tables. Because estimates presented in this report generally exclude "don't know," "refused," and other invalid responses, sample and sub-sample sizes (n's) vary from table to table.

Because the number of victims sufficient to reliably calculate estimates varies depending on the rarity of the exposure and the denominator of the subgroup being analyzed, the relative standard error (RSE) was calculated for each estimate presented. (RSE is the ratio of the standard error divided by the actual point estimate.) Estimates with RSEs that exceed 30 percent were deemed unstable and were not tested for statistically significant differences between or among groups. These estimates have been identified in the tables and should be viewed with caution.

Precision of Sample Estimates

The estimates generated from the NVAW Survey, as from any survey, are subject to random sampling error. Exhibit 1 presents the estimated standard errors multiplied by the z-score (1.96) for specified sample and subsample sizes of 16,000 or less at different response distributions of dichotomous variables (e.g., raped/not raped and injured/not injured). These estimated standard error by z-score combinations can be used to determine the extent to which sample estimates will be distributed around the population parameter (i.e., the true population distribution). As exhibit 1 shows, larger sample and subsample sizes produce smaller estimated standard errors at the 95-percent confidence level. Thus, the estimated 95-percent confidence interval for a sample or subsample size of 8,000 when the response distribution is a 50/50 split is 50 +/– 1.1 percent. For a sample or subsample size of 50, the 95-percent confidence interval is 50 +/– 14 percent.

Characteristics of the Sample and Sample Weighting

The NVAW Survey sample consists of 8,000 women and 8,000 men who were age 18 years or older and living in a U.S. household with a working residential telephone at the time of the interview. To determine the representative nature of the sample, select demographic characteristics of the NVAW Survey sample (e.g., age, race, Hispanic origin, marital status, and education) were compared with demographic characteristics of the general population as measured by the U.S. Census Bureau's 1995 Current Population Survey (CPS) of adult men and women (see exhibit 2). Estimates from the 1995 CPS were used because the NVAW Survey sample was generated in 1995.

As exhibit 2 shows, the demographic characteristics of the NVAW Survey sample are similar to the general population from which it was drawn. However, differences between point estimates from the NVAW Survey and those from the CPS are outside the expected margin of error (i.e., are not included in the 95-percent confidence interval computed from NVAW Survey estimates) for some demographic characteristics. Specifically, the NVAW Survey sample underrepresents older people, African-Americans, Hispanic men, and those with less than a high school education. To a lesser degree, those less than age 30 are also underrepresented. Complementary groups (e.g., the middle aged, whites, and the college educated) are overrepresented.

Tests were conducted to correct for possible biases introduced by the fact that some households had multiple telephone lines and multiple eligibles and for over- and underrepresentation of selected demographic subgroups. Although a few small but significant differences were observed for some outcome measures using weighted data, the researchers chose not to use weighted data in the analysis of the NVAW Survey data (see sidebar "Reasons for Using Unweighted Data" in this chapter).

Minimizing the Potential for Harming Respondents

Any form of research that involves contact with live persons, particularly those who may have been victims of violence, has the potential of resulting in harm to them. For this reason it is important that researchers carefully consider beforehand how their research might inadvertently harm their research subjects.

In the NVAW Survey, numerous techniques were used to protect the confidentiality of the information being gathered, minimize the potential for retraumatizing victims of violence, and minimize the potential for placing respondents in further danger:

- The researchers selected SRBI, an external contractor with extensive expertise conducting

	Women (%)		Men (%)	
Demographic Characteristic	NVAW Survey	U.S. Population	NVAW Survey	U.S. Population
Age[a]				
18–24	9.8	11.9	11.4	13.0
25–29	9.6	9.4	10.4	10.2
30–39	24.6	21.9	25.4	23.8
40–49	22.5	18.9	24.0	20.0
50–59	14.4	12.9	13.5	13.0
60–69	9.9	10.7	8.8	10.1
70–79	6.8	8.9	5.2	7.0
80 years +	2.5	5.5	1.5	2.9
Total Cases[b]	**7,856**		**7,920**	
Race[c]				
White	86.6	83.7	87.4	84.8
African-American	10.5	12.0	9.0	10.9
Native American/Alaska Native	1.2	0.7	1.4	0.7
Asian/Pacific Islander	1.8	3.6	2.2	3.5
Total Cases[b]	**7,453**		**7,353**	
Hispanic Origin (may be of any race)[c]				
Hispanic	7.9	8.5	7.3	9.4
Non-Hispanic	92.1	91.5	92.7	90.6
Total Cases[b]	**7,945**		**7,916**	
Marital Status[d]				
Never married	15.4	19.4	21.1	26.8
Currently married	62.9	59.2	66.9	62.7
Divorced, separated	13.2	10.3	10.2	8.03
Widowed	8.5	11.1	1.9	2.5
Total Cases[b]	**7,953**		**7,966**	
Education (persons 25 years or older)[d]				
Less than high school	10.7	18.4	9.4	18.3
High school and equivalent	34.6	35.7	29.3	31.9
Any college	45.7	39.7	48.3	40.4
Advanced degree	9.0	6.2	13.0	9.4
Total Cases[b]	**7,069**		**7,010**	

Exhibit 2. Comparison of Demographic Characteristics of NVAW Survey Sample and U.S. Population

[a]U.S. Population: Wetrogan, Signe I., *Projections of the Population of States by Age, Sex, and Race: 1988 to 2010*, Current Population Reports, P25–017, Washington, DC: U.S. Census Bureau, 1988.

[b]Due to nonresponse, NVAW case count totals vary across characteristics.

[c]U.S. Population: Day, Jennifer Cheeseman, *Population Projections of the United States by Age, Sex, Race, and Hispanic Origin: 1998 to 2050*, Current Population Reports, P25–104, Washington, DC: U.S. Census Bureau, 1993.

[d]U.S. Population: U.S. Census Bureau, *Statistical Abstract of the United States: 1996* (116th edition), Washington, DC: U.S. Census Bureau: 1996.

surveys on sensitive issues, to administer the survey. Because of this experience, SRBI was extremely cognizant of the need to protect the privacy, safety, and well-being of persons responding to the survey.

- Samples of working residential telephone numbers of potential respondents were generated using random-digit dialing. Thus, only a 10-digit telephone number linked the respondent to the interviewer. The area code and the first three digits of the telephone number were kept for analysis purposes; the last four digits of the number were eliminated from the dataset.

- The samples were programmed into a CATI system which brought up a telephone number

for the interviewer and automatically assigned the interview an identification number linked to the telephone number. All subsequent coding, data editing, and analysis were conducted using only the identification numbers.

- Interviewers were required to sign a confidentiality agreement that specified they would not reveal information about the respondents to anyone who was not involved with the project as an SRBI employee.

- During the introduction, respondents were told they would be asked about their personal experiences and opinions and that participation in the survey was completely voluntary.

- Respondents were given a toll-free number they could call to verify the legitimacy of the

Reasons for Using Unweighted Data

Several factors entered into the decision to not weight data for number of telephone lines, number of eligibles, and demographic characteristics:

- The differences between weighted and unweighted samples and outcomes were not large enough to make weighting mandatory.

- Weighting on multiple variables would have resulted in a few cases being heavily weighted, given their unique combination of demographic characteristics, telephone lines, and number of eligible respondents. Because portions of the NVAW Survey analysis were conducted using relatively small subgroups, there was an increased risk that the results would have been seriously affected by the responses of a few heavily weighted (and atypical) cases.

- The construction of demographic weights is complicated by the fact a "mixed race" category is included in the race question in the NVAW Survey but not the Census survey. Because the proportion of respondents who identified themselves as mixed race is substantial (5.7 percent for women and 6.0 percent for men) and decreases with age, treatment of the mixed race

respondents would have had a significant effect on weights for race. For example, assigning all of the mixed race respondents to a nonwhite status would have decreased the weighting of younger, nonwhite respondents. Therefore, the mixed race respondents were not included in the racial weighting. However, having a large percentage of respondents with an indeterminate race weighting makes an analysis using demographic weights subject to capricious interpretations.

- Weighting would have added an additional issue to an already complex data analysis. The NVAW Survey includes perpetrator-specific details of multiple incidents of victimization. This factor introduces an unusual level of complexity in the data and data analysis.

The *National Violence Against Women Survey Methodology Report* describes the survey methods and reports on sample characteristics and prevalence rates using weighted and unweighted data. (For ordering information, see "Other Publications From the National Violence Against Women Survey" in the executive summary.)

survey or to respond to the survey at a later date. Respondents were also told to use this number if they needed to suddenly hang up during the interview.

- If a respondent appeared to be in distress, interviewers were instructed to contact a supervisor who monitored the interview from that point and intervened as necessary. If necessary, the respondent was provided with a local rape or domestic violence hotline telephone number.

- At the end of the interview, respondents were asked if they had anything to add regarding the issues covered in the survey. They were also given a toll-free number to call if they had any further questions about the survey or wished to speak further about their experiences.

In addition to lessening the possibility that respondents would be harmed as a result of their participation in the survey, these techniques were likely to have improved the quality of the information being gathered. Some respondents, such as those who had never previously disclosed their victimization, may have benefitted from their participation in the survey.

Limitations of Telephone Surveys

By its nature, a telephone survey is limited to the population living in households with telephones. Thus, the survey does not reflect the experiences of women and men living in households without telephones, on the streets, or in group facilities or institutions. The absence of interviews with phoneless households results in an underrepresentation of certain demographic characteristics typical of such households (e.g., poor, headed by a single adult, located in a rural or inner city area, and renters).[9] Because approximately 94 percent of the American population lives in households with telephones,[10] this underrepresentation is relatively small.

Notes

1. SRBI is a New York City-based professional survey research firm. John Boyle, Ph.D., is senior vice president and director of SRBI's Government and Social Research Division. Dr. Boyle, who specializes in public policy research in the area of health and violence, also manages the firm's Washington, D.C.-area office.

2. The authors found a few small but statistically significant interviewer gender effects; see Tjaden, P., N. Thoennes, and C. Allison, "Effects of Interviewer Gender on Men's Responses to a Telephone Survey on Violent Victimization," *Journal of Quantitative Criminology* (forthcoming).

3. See National Victim Center and the Crime Victims Research and Treatment Center, *Rape in America: A Report to the Nation,* 211 Wilson Boulevard, Suite 300, Arlington, VA 22201, April 23, 1992: 15.

4. Straus, M.A., and R.J. Gelles, "Societal Change and Change in Family Violence From 1975 to 1986 as Revealed by Two National Studies," *Journal of Marriage and the Family* 48 (1986): 465–479.

5. Johnson, H., *Dangerous Domains: Violence Against Women in Canada*, Scarborough, Ontario: International Thomas Publishing, 1996.

6. Straus, M.A., "Measuring Intrafamily Conflict and Violence: The Conflict Tactics (CT) Scale," *Journal of Marriage and the Family* 41 (February 1979): 75–88.

7. National Criminal Justice Association, *Project to Develop a Model Anti-Stalking Code for States*, Washington, DC: U.S. Department of Justice, National Institute of Justice, 1993, NCJ 144477.

8. Tjaden, P., N. Thoennes, and C.J. Allison, "Comparing Stalking Victimization From Legal and Victim Perspectives," *Violence and Victims* 15 (1) (2000): 1–16.

9. Keeter, S., "Estimated Telephone Noncoverage Bias with a Telephone Survey," *Public Opinion Quarterly* 59 (1995): 196–217.

10. Ibid., p. 197; see also Lavrakas, P. J., *Telephone Survey Methods*, Second Edition, Newbury Park, CA: Sage Publications, 1993: 9.

3. Prevalence and Incidence of Rape, Physical Assault, and Stalking

This chapter examines the prevalence and incidence of rape, physical assault, and stalking among women and men in the United States. *Prevalence* refers to the number of *persons* within a demographic group (e.g., female or male) who are victimized during a specific time period, such as a person's lifetime or the previous 12 months. *Incidence* refers to the number of separate victimizations, or *incidents*, perpetrated against persons within a demographic group during a specific time period. Incidence expressed as a *victimization rate* is obtained by dividing the number of victimizations perpetrated against persons in a demographic group by the number of persons in the demographic group and setting the rate to a standard population base, such as 1,000 persons.[1]

Prevalence and Incidence of Rape

Using a definition of rape that included forced vaginal, oral, and anal sex, the survey found that 17.6 percent of surveyed women and 3.0 percent of surveyed men said they experienced a completed or attempted rape at some time in their life (see exhibit 3). Thus, 1 of 6 U.S. women and 1 of 33 U.S. men have been victims of a completed or attempted rape.

Relatively few women and men reported they were victims of an *attempted* rape only. While 14.8 percent of surveyed women said they had experienced a completed rape, 2.8 percent said they had experienced an attempted rape only. Similarly, while 2.1 percent of surveyed men said they had experienced a completed rape, 0.9 percent said they had experienced an attempted rape only. These findings indicate that most rapists successfully penetrate their victims.

Prior to the NVAW Survey, national information on rape occurring over the lifetime of the victim was limited to data on forced sex generated by two nationwide studies—the National Health and Social Life Survey and the National Women's Study. Findings from the NVAW Survey are similar to findings from these two previous surveys. The National Health and Social Life Survey found that 22 percent of surveyed women and 2 percent of surveyed men had been *forced to do something sexual* at some time in their life.[2] The National Women's Study found that 13 percent of surveyed women had been victims of a *completed forcible rape* at some time in their life.[3]

The NVAW Survey also found that 0.3 percent of women surveyed and 0.1 percent of men surveyed said they were raped in the previous 12 months.[4] These findings equate to an estimated 302,091 women and 92,748 men who are forcibly raped each year in the United States (see exhibit 4).

Because some rape victims experienced more than one rape in the previous 12 months, the *incidence* of rape (number of separate victimizations) exceeded the *prevalence* of rape (number of victims). Specifically, women who were raped in the previous 12 months averaged 2.9 rapes, while men averaged 1.2 rapes. According to survey estimates, 876,064 rapes were committed against women, and 111,298 rapes were committed against men in the previous 12 months (see exhibit 5). These figures equate respectively to an annual victimization rate of 8.7 rapes per 1,000 U.S. women age 18 and older [876,064 ÷ 100,697,000 = 0.0087 x 1,000 = 8.7] and an annual victimization rate of 1.2 rapes per 1,000 U.S. men age 18 and older [111,298 ÷ 92,748,000 = 0.0012 x 1,000 = 1.2].

Because annual rape victimization estimates are based on responses from only 24 women and

14

Exhibit 3. Persons Victimized in Lifetime by Type of Victimization and Victim Gender

Type of Victimization	Percentage		Number[a]	
	Women (n=8,000)	Men (n=8,000)	Women (100,697,000)	Men (92,748,000)
Total rape[b]	**17.6**	**3.0**	**17,722,672**	**2,782,440**
Completed[b]	14.8	2.1	14,903,156	1,947,708
Attempted only[b]	2.8	0.9	2,819,516	834,732
Total physical assault[b]	**51.9**	**66.4**	**52,261,743**	**61,584,672**
Threw something[b]	14.0	22.4	14,097,580	20,775,552
Pushed, grabbed, shoved[b]	30.6	43.5	30,813,282	40,345,380
Pulled hair	19.0	17.9	19,132,430	16,601,892
Slapped, hit[b]	43.0	53.7	43,299,710	49,805,676
Kicked, bit[b]	8.9	15.2	8,962,033	14,097,696
Choked, tried to drown[b]	7.7	3.9	7,753,669	3,617,172
Hit with object[b]	21.2	34.7	21,347,764	32,183,556
Beat up[c]	14.1	15.5	14,198,277	14,375,940
Threatened with gun[b]	6.2	13.1	6,243,214	12,149,988
Threatened with knife[b]	5.8	16.1	5,840,426	14,932,428
Used gun[b]	2.6	5.1	2,618,122	4,730,148
Used knife[b]	3.5	9.6	3,524,395	8,903,808
Rape and/or physical assault[b]	**55.0**	**66.8**	**55,383,350**	**61,955,664**
Stalking[b]	**8.1**	**2.2**	**8,156,457**	**2,040,456**
Any of the above[b]	**55.9**	**66.9**	**56,289,623**	**62,048,412**

[a]Based on estimates of women and men age 18 and older; U.S. Population: Wetrogan, Signe I., *Projections of the Population of States by Age, Sex, and Race: 1988 to 2010*, Current Population Reports, P25–1017, Washington, DC: U.S. Census Bureau, 1988.
[b]Differences between women and men are statistically significant: χ^2, p-value ≤ .001.
[c]Differences between women and men are statistically significant: χ^2, p-value ≤ .01.

Exhibit 4. Persons Victimized in Previous 12 Months by Type of Victimization and Victim Gender

Type of Victimization	Percentage		Number[a]	
	Women (n=8,000)	Men (n=8,000)	Women (100,697,000)	Men (92,748,000)
Rape	0.3	0.1[d]	302,091	92,748[d]
Physical assault[b]	1.9	3.4	1,913,243	3,153,432
Rape and/or physical assault[b]	2.1	3.5	2,114,637	3,246,180
Stalking[b]	1.0	0.4	1,006,970	370,992
Any of the above[c]	3.0	3.9	3,020,910	3,617,172

[a]Based on estimates of women and men age 18 and older, U.S. Population: Wetrogan, Signe I., *Projections of the Population of States by Age, Sex, and Race: 1988 to 2010*, Current Population Reports, P25–1017, Washington, DC: U.S. Census Bureau, 1988.
[b]Differences between women and men are statistically significant: χ^2, p-value ≤ .001.
[c]Differences between women and men are statistically significant: χ^2, p-value ≤ .01.
[d]Relative standard error exceeds 30 percent; statistical tests not performed.

	Estimated Number of Victims	Average Number of Victimizations per Victim[a]	Estimated Total Number of Victimizations	Annual Rate of Victimizations per 1,000 Persons
Type of Victimization				
Women				
Rape	302,091	2.9[b]	876,064[b]	8.7
Physical assault	1,913,243	3.1	5,931,053	58.9
Stalking	1,006,970	1.0	1,006,970	10.0
Men				
Rape	92,748[b]	1.2[b]	111,298[b]	1.2
Physical assault	3,153,432	2.5	7,883,580	85.0
Stalking	370,992	1.0	370,992	4.0

Exhibit 5. Estimated Number of Rape, Physical Assault, and Stalking Victimizations Perpetrated Annually by Victim Gender

[a] The standard error of the mean is 1.4 for female rape victims, 0.2 for female physical assault victims, 0.5 for male rape victims, and 0.2 for male physical assault victims. Because stalking by definition means repeated acts and because no victim was stalked by more than one perpetrator in the 12 months preceding the survey, the number of stalking victimizations was imputed to be the same as the number of stalking victims. Thus, the average number of stalking victimizations per victim is 1.0.

[b] Relative standard error exceeds 30 percent.

8 men who reported having been raped, they should be viewed with caution. Also, they probably underestimate the true number of rapes committed annually in the United States because they exclude attempted or completed rapes perpetrated against children and adolescents, as well as rapes perpetrated against women and men who were homeless or living in institutions, group facilities, or households without telephones.

NVAW Survey estimates of the number of rapes perpetrated against women and men annually (876,064 and 111,298, respectively) are higher than comparable estimates from the Bureau of Justice Statistics (BJS) National Crime Victimization Survey (NCVS). The NCVS estimates for 1994—a year that approximates the timeframe for the NVAW Survey—are 432,100 rapes or sexual assaults of U.S. females age 12 and older and 32,900 rapes or sexual assaults of U.S. males age 12 and older.[5]

It should be noted that direct comparisons between the two surveys are difficult to make because they differ substantially with respect to several methodological issues. First, the two surveys differ substantially with respect to

sample design and survey administration. The NVAW Survey was drawn by random-digit dialing from a database of households with a telephone (see chapter 2, "Survey Methods"). Moreover, NVAW Survey interviewers used state-of-the-art techniques to protect the confidentiality of their respondents and minimize the potential for retraumatizing victims of violence. In comparison, the NCVS sample consists of housing units (e.g., addresses) selected from a stratified multistage cluster sample. When a sample unit is selected for inclusion in the NCVS, U.S. Census workers interview all individuals in the household 12 years of age and older every 6 months for 3 years. Thus, after the first interview, respondents know the content of the survey. This may pose a problem for victims of family violence who may be afraid that disclosing violence by a family member may put them in further danger. It may also pose a problem for victims who do not want other family members to learn about their victimization. Although census interviewers document whether others were present during the interviews, time and budget constraints prevent them from ensuring privacy during an interview.

In addition, the NVAW Survey and the NCVS use substantially different rape screening questions. The NVAW Survey used five questions to screen respondents for rape victimization, while the NCVS used two questions.[6] Although empirical data on this issue are limited, some researchers assume that increasing the number of screening questions increases disclosure rates.[7] Furthermore, the NVAW Survey screening questions (see "Survey Screening Questions" in chapter 2) were more explicit than those used by the NCVS.

Another possible reason for the difference in NVAW Survey and NCVS findings is that published NCVS estimates count series victimizations—reports of six or more crimes within a 6-month period for which the respondent could not recall details of each crime—as a single victimization. Thus published NCVS estimates of the number of rapes and sexual assaults are lower than would be obtained by including all rapes and sexual assaults reported to its survey interviewers. To produce NCVS estimates for direct comparison with NVAW Survey estimates, each crime in a series of victimizations reported to the NCVS interviewers would have to be counted separately.

Finally, the sampling errors associated with the estimates from the NVAW Survey and the NCVS would have to be compared. This is particularly important given the relatively high margin of error associated with NVAW Survey estimates of the average number of rapes experienced by female victims annually (see footnote a in exhibit 5). Comparisons of sampling errors would help determine whether the estimates were truly different or whether apparent differences were not statistically significant.

A recent study funded by NIJ, BJS, and CDC provides more comprehensive information about the differences between the two surveys, including error ranges for the estimates. The study, which calculated annual rape and physical assault victimization estimates for women using data from the two surveys, the same counting rules, and the same age populations, found that

the number of rape victimizations uncovered by the NVAW Survey is significantly higher than estimates obtained from the NCVS. Specifically, the point estimate of the total number of rape victimizations experienced by adult women is larger for the NVAW Survey (876,064) compared with the NCVS (268,640). In addition, the 95-percent confidence intervals constructed around the point estimate for rape from the NVAW Survey (443,772 to 1,308,356) and the NCVS (193,110 to 344,170) do not overlap.[8]

Prevalence and Incidence of Physical Assault

The NVAW Survey used a modified version of the Conflict Tactics Scale[9] to query respondents about a wide range of physical assaults they may have experienced as children at the hands of adult caretakers (e.g., parents, stepparents, or legal guardians) and as adults at the hands of other adults. Responses revealed that physical assault is widespread in American society: 51.9 percent of surveyed women and 66.4 percent of surveyed men said they were physically assaulted by an adult caretaker as a child and/or by another adult as an adult (exhibit 3).

For both women and men the most frequently reported physical assault was slapping and hitting; followed by pushing, grabbing, and shoving; and hitting with an object. Relatively few respondents reported an adult caretaker or other adult pulled their hair or threw something that could hurt. Still fewer reported an adult caretaker or other adult choked or almost drowned them, kicked or bit them, beat them up, threatened them with a gun or knife, or used a gun or knife on them (see exhibit 3).

The authors know of no previous study that has examined women's and men's lifetime experiences with physical assault. Thus information from the NVAW Survey fills a serious gap in the research literature on violent victimization.

The NVAW Survey also found that 1.9 percent of surveyed women and 3.4 percent of surveyed men said they were physically assaulted in the previous 12 months. These estimates equate to about 1.9 million women and about 3.2 million men who are physically assaulted annually in the United States (see exhibit 4). Female victims averaged 3.1 assaults, and male victims averaged 2.5 assaults per year, which equate to approximately 5.9 million physical assaults perpetrated against women and 7.9 million physical assaults perpetrated against men in the previous 12 months (see exhibit 5). These figures represent an annual victimization rate of 58.9 physical assaults per 1,000 U.S. women age 18 and older [5,931,053 ÷ 100,697,000 = 0.0589 x 1,000 = 58.9] and an annual victimization rate of 85.0 physical assaults per 1,000 U.S. men aged 18 and older [7,883,580 ÷ 92,748,000 = 0.0850 x 1,000 = 85.0].

These estimates probably underestimate the number of physical assaults committed against women and men annually because the NVAW Survey categorized victimizations involving both rape and physical assault only as rapes (see "Rates of Physical Assault Among Rape Victims" in chapter 3). In addition, these estimates exclude physical assaults committed against children and adolescents by adult caretakers and siblings, against adolescents by other adolescents, and against women and men who were homeless or living in institutions, group facilities, or households without telephones.

NVAW Survey estimates of the number of physical assaults perpetrated against women and men annually (5.9 million and 7.9 million, respectively) are higher than comparable published NCVS estimates. The NCVS estimates for 1994 are 4.1 million simple and aggravated assaults of women age 12 and older and 5.7 million simple and aggravated assaults of men age 12 and older.[10] Comparisons between the NVAW Survey and NCVS estimates of physical assault are confounded by the same methodological difference discussed earlier and are addressed by a study funded by NIJ, BJS, and CDC (see "Prevalence and Incidence of Rape" in chapter 3). The study found that the NVAW Survey and the NCVS

appear to uncover statistically comparable levels of physical assault against adult women. While the point estimate of the total number of physical assault victimizations experienced by adult women is smaller for the NVAW Survey (5,931,053) compared with the NCVS (6,248,433), the 95-percent confidence intervals constructed around the point estimate for physical assault from the NVAW Survey (5,605,801 to 6,250,565) and the NCVS (5,948,656 to 6,548,210) overlap.[11]

Rates of Physical Assault Among Rape Victims

The NVAW Survey found that rape is often accompanied by physical assault: 41.4 percent of women and 33.9 percent of men who were raped since age 18 were physically assaulted during their most recent rape. The physical assaults included slapping, hitting, kicking, biting, choking, hitting with an object, beatings, and the use of a gun or other weapon.

Based on the estimated number of rapes perpetrated against women and men annually (exhibit 5), there are 362,690 rape-related physical assaults perpetrated against U.S. women annually [0.414 x 876,064 = 362,690] and 37,730 rape-related physical assaults perpetrated against U.S. men annually [0.339 x 111,298 = 37,730]. If these rape-related physical assaults are added to the number of physical assaults occurring annually (exhibit 5), the number of physical assaults perpetrated against U.S. women annually increases from 5,931,053 to 6,293,743 [5,931,053 + 362,690 = 6,293,743] and the number of physical assaults perpetrated against U.S. men annually increases from 7,883,580 to 7,921,310 [7,883,580 + 37,730 = 7,921,310]. These combined physical assault and rape-related physical assault estimates represent an annual victimization rate of 62.5 physical assaults per 1,000 U.S. women age 18 and older [6,293,743 ÷ 100,697,000 = 0.0625 x 1,000 = 62.5] and an annual victimization rate of 85.4 physical assaults per 1,000 U.S. men age 18 and older [7,921,310 ÷ 92,748,000 = 0.0854 x 1,000 = 85.4]. Again, because annual rape victimization estimates are based on responses from only 24 women and 8 men who reported having been raped, these estimates should be viewed with caution.

Prevalence and Incidence of Stalking

Although it uses a definition of stalking that requires victims to feel a high level of fear, the NVAW Survey found that stalking is much more prevalent than previously thought: 8.1 percent of surveyed women and 2.2 percent of surveyed men said they were stalked at some time in their life (exhibit 3). The survey also found that 1.0 percent of surveyed women and 0.4 percent of surveyed men said they were stalked in the previous 12 months. Based on U.S. Census estimates of the number of women and men in the country, approximately 1 million women and 371,000 men are stalked annually in the United States (exhibit 4). Because these figures exclude cases involving victims less than 18 years old, as well as victims who are homeless or living in institutions, group facilities, or households without telephones, they probably underestimate the true number of Americans who are stalked each year.

If a less stringent definition of stalking is used—one requiring victims to feel somewhat frightened or a little frightened by their assailant's behavior—stalking prevalence rates increase dramatically for both women and men. Specifically, lifetime stalking prevalence rates increase from 8.1 to 12.0 percent for women and 2.2 to 4.0 percent for men; annual stalking prevalence rates increase from 1.0 to 6.0 percent for women and 0.4 to 1.5 percent for men. Based on these higher prevalence estimates, approximately 12.1 million women and 3.7 million men are stalked at some time in their life, and about 6 million women and 1.4 million men are stalked annually.

Because stalking by definition involves repeated acts of harassment and intimidation and because no victim was stalked by more than one perpetrator in the 12 months preceding the survey, the *incidence* (number of separate victimizations) of

stalking is equal to the *prevalence* (number of victims) of stalking. Thus the annual stalking victimization rate is 10.0 stalkings per 1,000 U.S. women [1,006,970 ÷ 100,697,000 = 0.0100 x 1,000 = 10.0] and 4.0 stalkings per 1,000 U.S. men [370,990 ÷ 92,748,000 = 0.0040 x 1,000 = 4.0] (see exhibit 5).

Prior to the NVAW Survey, information on stalking prevalence was limited to guesses provided by forensic specialists and mental health professionals based on their work with known stalkers. The most frequently cited "guesstimates" of stalking prevalence were made by forensic psychiatrist Park Dietz, who in 1992 reported that 5 percent of U.S. women are stalked at some time in their life, and approximately 200,000 U.S. women are stalked each year.[12] The NVAW Survey estimate that 8.1 percent of U.S. women have been stalked at some time in their life is 1.6 times greater than Dietz's earlier, nonscientific estimate, and the survey's estimate that 1,006,970 U.S. women are stalked annually is 5 times greater.

Notes

1. Koss, M.R., and M.A. Harvey, *The Rape Victim: Clinical and Community Interventions,* Second Edition, Newbury Park, CA: Sage Publications, 1991.

2. Michael, R.T., J.H. Gagnon, E.O. Laumann, and G. Kolata, *Sex in America: A Definitive Survey,* New York: Warner Books, 1994.

3. National Victim Center and the Crime Victims Research and Treatment Center, *Rape in America: A Report to the Nation,* 211 Wilson Boulevard, Suite 300, Arlington, VA 22201, April 23, 1992: 15.

4. The NVAW Survey was conducted from November 1995 to May 1996. Respondents reported on events that spanned the 12 months prior to their interview. Thus, a person who was interviewed in November 1995 reported on events that occurred between November 1994 and November 1995; a person who was interviewed in May 1996 reported on events that occurred between May 1995 and May 1996.

5. Craven, D., *Sex Differences in Violent Victimization, 1994,* Special Report, Washington, DC: U.S. Department of Justice, Bureau of Justice Statistics, 1997, NCJ 164508.

6. See "Survey Screening Questions," for the five NVAW questions on rape/sexual assault. The two questions used in the NCVS are as follows: *(1) (Other than any incidents already mentioned), has anyone attacked or threatened you in any of these ways . . . (e) Any rape, attempted rape, or other type of sexual attack? (2) (Other than any incident already mentioned), have you been forced or coerced to engage in unwanted sexual activity by (a) someone you didn't know before, (b) a casual acquaintance, or (c) someone you know well?*

7. For example, Koss, M.P., "Detecting the Scope of Rape: A Review of Prevalence Research Methods," *Journal of Interpersonal Violence* 8 (2) (June 1993): 198–222.

8. Bachman, R., "A Comparison of Annual Incidence Rates and Contextual Characteristics of Intimate-Partner Violence Against Women From the National Crime Victimization Survey (NCVS) and the National Violence Against Women Survey (NVAWS)," *Violence Against Women* 6 (8) (August 2000): 839–867.

9. Straus, M.A., "Measuring Intrafamily Conflict and Violence: The Conflict Tactics (CT) Scale," *Journal of Marriage and the Family* 41 (February 1979): 75–88.

10. Craven, *Sex Differences in Violent Victimization, 1994* (see note 5).

11. Bachman, "A Comparison of Annual Incidence Rates" (see note 8).

12. Although testimony provided at the September 29, 1992, Senate Judiciary Committee Hearing on the Violence Against Women bill (S. 2922) is generally cited as the source for these estimates, the figures first appeared in a *USA Today* article on stalking. See Maria Puente, "Legislators Tackling the Terror of Stalking: But Some Experts Say Measures Are Vague," *USA Today,* July 21, 1992.

4. Risk of Violence Among Racial Minorities and Hispanics

Estimates from the Bureau of Justice Statistics (BJS) National Crime Victimization Survey (NCVS) consistently show that African-Americans are at greater risk of victimization by violent crime than are whites or persons of other racial groupings and that Hispanics are at greater risk of violent victimization than are non-Hispanics. For example, the overall 1996 violent victimization rate per 1,000 persons age 12 and older reported by NCVS was 52.3 for blacks, 40.9 for whites, and 33.2 for persons designated "other," while the rate was 44.0 for Hispanics and 41.6 for non-Hispanics.[1] Typically, BJS does not publish information on victimization rates for other minorities, such as Native Americans, Asians, or persons who consider themselves mixed race.[2]

To generate information on violent victimization among women and men of diverse racial backgrounds, the NVAW Survey asked respondents whether they would best classify themselves as white, African-American, Asian or Pacific Islander, American Indian or Alaska Native, or mixed race. Respondents also were asked whether they were of Hispanic origin. The response rate on each question was very high: 98 percent of the women and 97 percent of the men answered the question about race, while 99 percent of both women and men answered the question about Hispanic origin.

This chapter examines the lifetime prevalence of rape, physical assault, and stalking among women and men of different racial backgrounds and between Hispanics and non-Hispanics. It begins with a comparison of victimization rates between women and men based on white/nonwhite status. This is followed by a comparison of prevalence rates among women and men of white, African-American, Asian/Pacific Islander, American Indian/Alaska Native, and mixed race backgrounds. Finally, a comparison is made between women and men of Hispanic and non-Hispanic origin.

Prevalence of Violence Among Whites and Nonwhites

When data on African-American, American Indian/Alaska Native, Asian/Pacific Islander, and mixed race women are combined, there is very little difference between white women and nonwhite women in rape, physical assault, or stalking prevalence: 17.7 percent of white women and 19.8 percent of nonwhite women reported they had experienced a completed or attempted rape at some time in their life; 51.3 percent of white women and 54 percent of nonwhite women reported they had been physically assaulted by an adult caretaker as a child and/or by another adult as an adult; and 8.2 percent of both white and nonwhite women reported they had been stalked at some time in their life (see exhibit 6).

Similarly, there were no significant differences between white men and nonwhite men with respect to reports of rape, physical assault, and stalking victimization (exhibit 6). These findings suggest that racial minority women and men are not at greater risk of violent victimization than are white women and men; however, they tell us little about the rate of violent victimization among women and men of diverse racial minority backgrounds.

Prevalence of Violence Among Specific Racial Minorities

A comparison of the prevalence of rape, physical assault, and stalking among women and men of specific racial groupings produced some interesting findings. First, data on victimization rates among women of diverse racial backgrounds

Exhibit 6. Persons Victimized in Lifetime by Type of Victimization, Victim Gender, and White/Nonwhite Status of Victim			
	Persons Victimized in Lifetime (%)		
Type of Victimization	Total	White	Nonwhite
Women	(*n*=7,850)	(*n*=6,452)	(*n*=1,398)
Rape	18.2	17.7	19.8
Physical assault	51.8	51.3	54.0
Stalking	8.2	8.2	8.2
Men	(*n*=7,759)	(*n*=6,424)	(*n*=1,335)
Rape	3.0	2.8	3.4
Physical assault	66.6	66.5	67.3
Stalking	2.3	2.1	3.0

Exhibit 7. Persons Victimized in Lifetime by Type of Victimization, Victim Gender, and Race						
	Persons Victimized in Lifetime (%)					
Type of Victimization	Total	White	African-American	Asian/Pacific Islander	American Indian/Alaska Native	Mixed Race
Women	(*n*=7,850)	(*n*=6,452)	(*n*=780)	(*n*=133)	(*n*=88)	(*n*=397)
Rape[a]	18.2	17.7	18.8	6.8[e]	34.1	24.4
Physical assault	51.8	51.3	52.1	49.6	61.4	57.7
Stalking[b]	8.2	8.2	6.5	4.5[e]	17.0	10.6
Men	(*n*=7,759)	(*n*=6,424)	(*n*=659)	(*n*=165)	(*n*=105)	(*n*=406)
Rape	3.0	2.8	3.3	___[d]	___[d]	4.4
Physical assault[c]	66.6	66.5	66.3	58.8	75.2	70.2
Stalking[a]	2.3	2.1	2.4	___[d]	___[d]	3.9

[a]Differences between white women and American Indian/Alaska Native, between African-American women and American Indian/Alaska Native women, and between white women and mixed-race women are statistically significant: Tukey's B, *p*-value ≤ .05.

[b]Differences between American Indian/Alaska Native women and white and African-American women are statistically significant: Tukey's B, *p*-value ≤ .05.

[c]Differences between American Indian/Alaska Native men and Asian/Pacific Islander men are statistically significant: Tukey's B, *p*-value ≤ .05.

[d]Estimates have not been calculated on fewer than five victims.

[e]Relative standard error exceeds 30 percent; statistical tests not performed.

showed that different types of minority women reported significantly different rates of victimization. For example, American Indian/Alaska Native women were significantly more likely than white women or African-American women to report they were raped. They were also significantly more likely than white women or African-American women to report they were stalked. In addition, mixed-race women were significantly more likely than white women to

report they were raped. Unfortunately, the small number of Asian/Pacific Islander women who reported they were raped and stalked made it impossible to test for statistically significant differences between them and women from other racial backgrounds (see exhibit 7).

The survey also found that American Indian/Alaska Native men reported significantly more physical assault victimization than did Asian/

Pacific Islander men. However, they did not report significantly more physical assaults than white men or men from other minority backgrounds (exhibit 7).

These findings underscore the need for specificity when comparing victimization rates among women and men of different racial backgrounds. As results from the survey show, combining data on all types of minorities may diminish differences that exist between whites and nonwhites and at the same time obscure very large differences in prevalence rates among women and men of specific racial backgrounds.

Findings from the NVAW Survey that show American Indians/Alaska Natives are at greater risk of violent victimization than are other Americans support findings from previous studies. A recent study by the Bureau of Justice Statistics found that the rate of violent victimization for Native Americans was more than twice the rate for the Nation (124 versus 50 per 1,000 persons age 12 and older).[3] A study by the National Center for Injury Prevention and Control found that homicide rates for Native Americans were about two times greater than U.S. national rates.[4] Another study using data from the 1985 National Family Violence Survey found that Native American couples were significantly more violent than their white counterparts.[5] Thus, there is some empirical evidence that Native Americans are at significantly greater risk of violence—fatal and nonfatal—than other Americans.

Because data on violence against American Indians and Alaska Natives are limited, it is difficult to explain why they report more victimization. How much of the variance in violent victimization that may be explained by demographic, social, and environmental factors remains unclear and requires further study. Moreover, there may be significant differences in the prevalence of rape, physical assault, and stalking victimization between American Indians and Alaska Natives that cannot be determined from

the survey because data on these two groups were combined. Finally, there may be significant differences in rates of violent victimization among women and men of diverse American Indian tribes and Alaska Native communities.

Because of the small numbers of Asian/Pacific Islander women and men who reported rape and stalking victimization, it is unclear whether they report significantly less victimization. It has been suggested that traditional Asian values emphasizing close family ties and harmony may discourage Asian women from disclosing violent victimization, especially by intimate partners.[6] The smaller victimization rates found among Asian/Pacific Islander women and men may be, at least in part, an artifact of underreporting. There also may be significant differences in victimization rates between Asian and Pacific Islander women and men that cannot be determined from the survey because data on these two groups were combined. Clearly, more research is needed on victimization among Asian and Pacific Islander women and men and how their victimization experiences compare with those of women and men from other racial and ethnic backgrounds.

Prevalence of Violence Among Hispanics and Non-Hispanics

The NVAW Survey found that women who identified themselves as Hispanic were significantly less likely to report they had ever been raped than women who identified themselves as non-Hispanic (see exhibit 8). However, Hispanic women and non-Hispanic women were nearly equally likely to report physical assault or stalking victimization. Because previous studies comparing the prevalence of violence among Hispanic and non-Hispanic women have produced contradictory conclusions,[7] findings from the NVAW Survey neither support nor contradict earlier findings.

The survey found no significant differences in rape, physical assault, or stalking victimization

Exhibit 8. Persons Victimized in Lifetime by Type of Victimization, Victim Gender, and Hispanic/Non-Hispanic Origin			
	Persons Victimized in Lifetime (%)		
Type of Victimization	Total	Hispanic[a]	Non-Hispanic
Women	**(n=7,945)**	**(n=628)**	**(n=7,317)**
Rape[b]	18.1	14.6	18.4
Physical assault	51.9	53.2	51.8
Stalking	8.1	7.6	8.2
Men	**(n=7,916)**	**(n=581)**	**(n=7,335)**
Rape	3.0	3.4	3.0
Physical assault	66.5	63.2	66.8
Stalking	2.2	3.3	2.1
[a]Persons of Hispanic origin may be of any race.			
[b]Differences between Hispanics and non-Hispanics are statistically significant: p-value ≤ .05.			

rates between Hispanic and non-Hispanic men (exhibit 8). These findings contradict findings from the NCVS that show Hispanics are at greater risk of violent victimization than non-Hispanics.[8]

Notes

1. Ringel, C., *Criminal Victimization 1996: Changes 1995–96 With Trends 1993–96*, Washington, DC: U.S. Department of Justice, Bureau of Justice Statistics, 1997, NCJ 165812.

2. The exception to this rule is a recent BJS report that focuses on violence against Native Americans; see Greenfeld, L.A., and S.K. Smith, *American Indians and Crime*, Washington, DC: U.S. Department of Justice, Bureau of Justice Statistics, 1999, NCJ 173386.

3. Ibid.

4. Wallace, L.J.D., A.D. Calhoun, K.E. Powell, J. O'Neil, and S.P. James, *Homicide and Suicide Among Native Americans, 1979–1992*, Violence Surveillance Summary Series, No. 2, Atlanta, GA: National Center for Injury Prevention and Control, 1996.

5. Bachman, R., *Death and Violence on the Reservation: Homicide, Family Violence, and Suicide in American Indian Populations*, Westport, CT: Auburn House, 1992.

6. National Research Council, *Understanding Violence Against Women*, Washington, DC: National Academy Press, 1966: 40–41.

7. See, for example, Sorenson, S.B., J.A. Stein, J.M. Siegel, J.M. Golding, and M.A. Burnam, "The Prevalence of Adult Sexual Assault: The Los Angeles Epidemiologic Catchment Area Project," *American Journal of Epidemiology* 126 (1987): 1154–1164; Sorenson, S.B., and C.A. Telles, "Self-Reports of Spousal Violence in a Mexican-American and a Non-Hispanic White Population," *Violence and Victims* 6 (1991): 3–16.

8. Ringel, *Criminal Victimization 1996* (see note 1).

5. Women's and Men's Risk of Intimate Partner Violence

Ever since Straus reported his controversial finding in 1977 that women are as violent as men toward their partners,[1] social scientists have debated the relative risk of male-to-female and female-to-male intimate partner violence. On one side of the debate are those who argue women and men are equally victimized by their intimate partners.[2] Evidence in support of this position comes primarily from surveys of married and cohabiting couples that ask respondents to self-report violent acts they have committed against their partners and violent acts they have sustained at the hands of their partners. On the other side of the debate are those who contend that women are at far greater risk of intimate partner violence than are men.[3] Evidence in support of this position comes primarily from national crime surveys and police, hospital, court, and clinical and shelter sample surveys that show women are overwhelmingly the victims of partner violence.

This chapter uses NVAW Survey data to compare the risk of intimate partner violence among women and men in the United States. Intimate partner victimization estimates are presented in terms of prevalence and incidence. As previously noted, *prevalence* refers to the number of persons within a demographic group (e.g., female or male) who are victimized during a specific time period, such as a person's lifetime or the previous 12 months. *Incidence* refers to the number of separate victimizations, or incidents, perpetrated against persons within a demographic group during a specific time period. The definition of intimate partner includes current or former spouses, opposite-sex cohabiting partners, same-sex cohabiting partners, boyfriends/girlfriends, and dates.

Prevalence and Incidence of Intimate Partner Violence

The NVAW Survey found that women were significantly more likely than men to report being victimized by an intimate partner, whether the time period covered was the individual's lifetime or the previous 12 months and whether the type of victimization considered was rape, physical assault, or stalking.

Intimate partner rape

Using a definition of rape that includes forced vaginal, oral, and anal sex that was completed or attempted (see "Survey Screening Questions" in chapter 2), the survey found that 7.7 percent of surveyed women and 0.3 percent of surveyed men were raped by a current or former intimate partner at some time in their life, while 0.2 percent of surveyed women were raped by a current or former intimate partner in the previous 12 months (see exhibit 9). Based on U.S. Census estimates of the number of women age 18 and older, 201,394 U.S. women are raped by an intimate partner annually in the United States. (The number of male rape victims ($n<5$) was insufficient to reliably calculate annual prevalence estimates for men.)

Because women raped by an intimate partner in the previous 12 months averaged 1.6 rapes, the incidence (number of separate victimizations) of intimate partner rapes exceeded the prevalence (number of victims) of intimate partner rape. Thus, there were an estimated 322,230 intimate partner rapes committed against U.S. women in the 12 months preceding the survey. This figure equates to an annual victimization rate of 3.2 intimate partner rapes per 1,000 U.S.

Exhibit 9. Persons Victimized by an Intimate Partner[a] in Lifetime and Previous 12 Months by Type of Victimization				
	In Lifetime			
	Percentage		Number[b]	
Type of Victimization	Women (*n*=8,000)	Men (*n*=8,000)	Women (100,697,000)	Men (92,748,000)
Rape[c]	7.7	0.3	7,753,669	278,244
Physical assault[c]	22.1	7.4	22,254,037	6,863,352
Rape and/or physical assault[c]	24.8	7.6	24,972,856	7,048,848
Stalking[c]	4.8	0.6	4,833,456	556,488
Total victimized[c]	25.5	7.9	25,677,735	7,327,092
	In Previous 12 Months			
Rape	0.2	___[e]	201,394	___[e]
Physical assault[d]	1.3	0.9	1,309,061	834,732
Rape and/or physical assault[c]	1.5	0.9[f]	1,510,455	834,732[f]
Stalking[c]	0.5	0.2	503,485	185,496
Total victimized[c]	1.8	1.1	1,812,546	1,020,228

[a]Intimate partners include current and former spouses, opposite-sex and same-sex cohabiting partners, boyfriends/girlfriends, and dates.

[b]Based on estimates of women and men age 18 and older, U.S. Population: Wetrogan, Signe I., *Projections of the Population of States by Age, Sex, and Race: 1988 to 2010*, Current Population Reports, Washington, DC: U.S. Bureau of the Census, 1988: 25–1017.

[c]Differences between women and men are statistically significant: χ^2, *p*-value $\leq$ .001.

[d]Differences between women and men are statistically significant: χ^2, *p*-value $\leq$ .05.

[e]Estimates have not been calculated on fewer than five victims.

[f]Because only three men reported being raped by an intimate partner in the previous 12 months, the percentage and estimated total number of men physically assaulted and raped and/or physically assaulted is the same.

women aged 18 years and older [322,230 ÷ 100,697,000 = 0.0032 x 1,000 = 3.2] (see exhibit 10). (Because annual intimate partner rape estimates are based on responses from only 16 women who reported having been raped, they should be viewed with caution.)

Intimate partner physical assault

Using a definition of physical assault that includes a range of behaviors, from slapping and hitting to using a gun ("Survey Screening Questions" in chapter 2), the survey found that the most frequently reported intimate partner violence by far was physical assault: 22.1 percent of surveyed women and 7.4 percent of surveyed men said they were physically assaulted by an intimate partner at some time in their lifetime (exhibit 9). Thus, 1 out of every 5 U.S. women has been physically assaulted by an intimate part-

ner, compared with 1 out of every 14 U.S. men. The survey also found that 1.3 percent of surveyed women, compared with 0.9 percent of surveyed men, were physically assaulted by a current or former intimate partner in the previous 12 months. About 1.3 million women and 835,000 men are physically assaulted by an intimate partner annually in the United States (exhibit 9).

Because women who were physically assaulted by an intimate partner in the previous 12 months averaged 3.4 physical assaults, there were approximately 4.5 million physical assaults committed against U.S. women by intimate partners in the 12 months preceding the survey. This figure equates to an annual victimization rate of 44.2 intimate partner physical assaults per 1,000 U.S. women age 18 and older [4,450,807 ÷ 100,697,000 = 0.0442 x 1,000 = 44.2] (see exhibit 10).

The survey found that men who were physically assaulted by an intimate partner in the previous 12 months averaged 3.5 assaults. Thus, there were about 2.9 million physical assaults perpetrated against U.S. men by intimate partners in the previous 12 months. This figure equates to an annual victimization rate of 31.5 intimate partner physical assaults per 1,000 U.S. men age 18 and older [2,921,562 ÷ 92,748,000 = 0.0315 x 1,000 = 31.5] (exhibit 10).

Results from the survey show that most physical assaults perpetrated against women and men by intimate partners consist of pushing, grabbing, shoving, slapping, and hitting. Although assaults such as these may be considered relatively minor compared with other types (e.g., choking or being beaten up), serious injury can occur in some circumstances. For example, a woman or man who is pushed down the stairs could suffer a concussion or even death, while a woman or man who is slapped or hit could suffer a perforated eardrum or an eye injury.

Fewer women and men reported a current or former intimate partner threw something at them that could hurt, pulled their hair, kicked or beat them, or threatened them with a knife or gun compared with those who pushed, grabbed, shoved, slapped, or hit them. Only a negligible number reported that an intimate partner used a knife or gun on them (see exhibit 11).

It is important to note that differences between women's and men's rates of physical assault by an intimate partner become greater as the seriousness of the assault increases. For example, women were two to three times more likely than men to report that an intimate partner threw something at them that could hurt or pushed, grabbed, or shoved them. However, they were 7 to 14 times more likely to report that an intimate partner beat them up, choked or tried to drown them, or threatened them with a gun (exhibit 11).

Intimate partner stalking

Using a definition of stalking that requires victims to feel a high level of fear, the survey found that 4.8 percent of surveyed women and 0.6 percent of surveyed men were stalked by a current or former intimate partner at some time in their lifetime; 0.5 percent of surveyed women and 0.2 percent of surveyed men were stalked by a current or former intimate partner in the

Exhibit 10. Estimated Number of Rape, Physical Assault, and Stalking Victimizations Perpetrated by Intimate Partners Annually by Victim Gender				
Victim Gender	Estimated Number of Victims	Average Number of Victimizations per Victim[a]	Estimated Total Number of Victimizations	Annual Rate of Victimization per 1,000 Persons
Women				
Rape	201,394	1.6[b]	322,230[b]	3.2
Physical assault	1,309,061	3.4	4,450,807	44.2
Stalking	503,485	1.0	503,485	5.0
Men				
Rape[c]	—	—	—	—
Physical assault	834,732	3.5	2,921,562	31.5
Stalking	185,496	1.0	185,496	1.8

[a]The standard error of the mean is 0.5 for female rape victims, 0.6 for female physical assault victims, and 0.6 for male physical assault victims. Because stalking by definition means repeated acts and because no victim was stalked by more than one perpetrator in the 12 months preceding the survey, the number of stalking victimizations was imputed to be the same as the number of stalking victims. Thus, the average number of stalking victimizations per victim is 1.0.

[b]Relative standard error exceeds 30 percent.

[c]Estimates have not been calculated on fewer than five victims.

	Exhibit 11. Persons Physically Assaulted by an Intimate Partner[a] in Lifetime by Type of Assault and Victim Gender	
Type of Assault[b]	Women (%) (n=8,000)	Men (%) (n=8,000)
Total Reporting Physical Assault by Intimate Partner	22.1	7.4
Threw something that could hurt	8.1	4.4
Pushed, grabbed, shoved	18.1	5.4
Pulled hair	9.1	2.3
Slapped, hit	16.0	5.5
Kicked, bit	5.5	2.6
Choked, tried to drown	6.1	0.5
Hit with object	5.0	3.2
Beat up	8.5	0.6
Threatened with gun	3.5	0.4
Threatened with knife	2.8	1.6
Used gun	0.7	0.1[c]
Used knife	0.9	0.8

[a]Intimate partners include current and former spouses, opposite-sex and same-sex cohabiting partners, boyfriends/girlfriends, and dates.

[b]With the exception of "used gun" and "used knife," differences between females and males are statistically significant: χ^2, p-value $\leq$ .001.

[c]Relative standard error exceeds 30 percent; statistical tests not performed.

previous 12 months (exhibit 9). Based on U.S. Census Bureau estimates of the number of women and men in the country, 503,485 women and 185,496 men are stalked by an intimate partner annually in the United States.

Because stalking by definition involves repeated acts of harassment and intimidation, the *incidence* (number of separate victimizations) of intimate partner stalking is equal to the *prevalence* (number of victims) of intimate partner stalking. Thus, there were an estimated 503,485 stalking incidents perpetrated against women and 185,496 stalking incidents perpetrated against men by intimates in the year preceding the survey. These figures equate respectively to an annual victimization rate of 5 intimate partner stalkings per 1,000 U.S. women age 18 and older [503,485 ÷ 100,697,000 = 0.005 x 1,000 = 5.0] and 1.8 intimate partner stalkings per 1,000 U.S. men aged 18 years and older [185,496 ÷ 97,748,000 = 0.0018 x 1,000 = 1.8] (exhibit 10).

Comparison With Previous Research

Lifetime prevalence

Prior to the NVAW Survey, national information on women's and men's lifetime experiences with intimate partner rape was minimal. However, two community-based surveys provide data with which NVAW Survey estimates of the lifetime prevalence of intimate partner rape for women can be compared. A study of 930 San Francisco women found that 8 percent were survivors of marital rape,[4] while another study of 323 ever-married/cohabited women in Boston found that 10 percent were survivors of spousal or partner rape.[5] The NVAW Survey finding that 7.7 percent of U.S. women have been raped by an intimate partner at some time in their lifetime is similar to these earlier, community-based estimates.

Several community-based studies have examined women's and/or men's lifetime experiences with physical assaults by intimates. Survey estimates vary from 9 to 30 percent for women[6] and from 13 to 16 percent for men.[7] In addition, a 1997 Gallup Poll, which surveyed a nationally representative sample of 434 U.S. women and 438 U.S. men age 18 and older by telephone, found that 22 percent of the women and 8 percent of the men had ever been physically abused by their spouse or companion.[8] NVAW Survey estimates that 22.1 percent of U.S. women and 7.4 percent of U.S. men have been physically assaulted by an intimate partner at some time in their lifetime fall between lifetime prevalence estimates for women and men generated by earlier community-based surveys and are nearly identical to lifetime prevalence estimates for women and men from the Gallup Poll.

Annual prevalence and incidence

Previous information on women's and men's *annual* experiences with intimate partner violence comes from two main sources: the annual Bureau of Justice Statistics (BJS) National Crime Victimization Survey (NCVS) and the National Family Violence Survey (NFVS), which was first conducted in 1975 and subsequently reconducted in 1985. Portions of the NFVS were also included in the 1992 National Alcohol and Family Violence Survey and a special component of the 1995 National Alcohol Survey.

Annual intimate partner victimization rates generated by the NCVS are substantially *lower* than those generated by the NVAW Survey. One study based on 1992–93 NCVS data found that the average annual rate of rape and sexual assault by an intimate was 1.0 per 1,000 women age 12 and older, while the combined annual rate of simple and aggravated assault by an intimate was 7.6 per 1,000 women age 12 and older and 1.3 per 1,000 men age 12 and older.[9] A more recent BJS study that used 1996 NCVS and Federal Bureau of Investigation data—which combined data on intimate partner murder, rape, sexual assault, robbery, and aggravated and simple assault—found that the annual rate of violent victimization by an intimate was 7.5

per 1,000 women age 12 and older and 1.4 per 1,000 men age 12 and older.[10] In comparison, the NVAW Survey annual rate of forcible rape by an intimate was 3.2 per 1,000 women age 18 and older, while the NVAW Survey annual rate of physical assault by an intimate was 44.2 per 1,000 women age 18 and older and 31.5 per 1,000 men age 18 and older.

On the other hand, annual intimate partner violence prevalence estimates generated by the NFVS are substantially *higher* than those generated by the NVAW Survey. The 1975 and 1985 NFVS found that 11 to 12 percent of married/cohabiting women and 12 percent of married/cohabiting men were physically assaulted by an intimate partner annually.[11] The 1992 National Alcohol and Family Violence Survey, which included parts of the NFVS, found that approximately 1.9 percent of married/cohabiting women were severely assaulted by a male partner annually and approximately 4.5 percent of married/cohabiting men were severely assaulted by a female partner annually.[12] The 1995 National Alcohol Survey, which also included parts of the NFVS, found that 5.2 to 13.6 percent of married/cohabiting couples experienced male-to-female partner violence annually and 6.2 to 18.2 percent of married/cohabiting couples experienced female-to-male intimate partner violence annually.[13]

In comparison, the NVAW Survey found that only 1.3 percent of all women and 0.9 percent of all men were physically assaulted by any type of intimate partner annually (exhibit 9). Moreover, the NVAW Survey uncovered similarly low rates of intimate partner violence when only responses from married/cohabiting respondents were considered. A recent study based on NVAW Survey data that focused specifically on physical assaults perpetrated by marital/cohabiting partners, and is therefore more directly comparable to NFVS findings, revealed that only 1.1 percent of married/cohabiting U.S. women and 0.6 percent of married/cohabiting U.S. men were physically assaulted by an intimate partner annually.[14]

The disparity in NFVS and NVAW Survey findings is particularly striking because both surveys used behaviorally specific questions included in the Conflict Tactics Scale to screen respondents for physical assault victimization.

The NVAW Survey finding that women are significantly more likely than men to be victimized by intimate partners contradicts results from the NFVS, which found that men and women are nearly equally likely to be physically assaulted by spouses or partners.[15] However, the NVAW Survey supports results from studies using NCVS data, which have consistently shown that women are at significantly greater risk of intimate partner violence.[16]

Deciphering Disparities in Survey Findings

It is difficult to explain why the NCVS, NFVS, and NVAW Survey generated such different annual intimate partner victimization rates or why the NFVS produced evidence of symmetry in women's and men's risk of intimate partner violence while the NCVS and NVAW Survey produced evidence of asymmetry. For years researchers have attributed the low rate of intimate partner violence uncovered by the NCVS to the fact it is administered in the context of a crime survey. Because they reflect only violence perpetrated by intimates that victims label as criminal and report to interviewers, estimates of intimate partner violence generated from the NCVS are thought to underestimate the true amount of intimate partner violence.[17]

At first glance, results from the NVAW Survey appear to support this theory: The NVAW Survey, which was administered in the context of a survey on personal safety and avoided legalistic phrases such as crime, rape, and physical assault, generated intimate partner violence victimization rates that are substantially higher than those from the NCVS. It is possible, however, that factors other than the context in which the two surveys were administered account for

some of the differences in their findings. As previously noted (see chapter 3, "Prevalence and Incidence of Rape, Physical Assault, and Stalking"), the NCVS and NVAW Survey differ substantially with respect to sample design, survey administration, interviewing techniques, screening questions, counting rules, age populations, and sampling errors. To produce NCVS estimates that are more directly comparable to NVAW Survey estimates, these factors would have to be controlled. A recent study funded by NIJ, BJS, and CDC, which calculated rape and physical assault estimates from the two surveys using the same counting rules and the same age populations, found that the NVAW Survey appears to uncover statistically higher levels of rape against adult women. However, the two surveys appear to uncover statistically comparable levels of physical assault against adult women.[18]

Differences between NVAW Survey and NFVS estimates are somewhat harder to explain because both surveys used questions from the Conflict Tactics Scale to screen respondents for intimate partner physical assault and similar sampling techniques. Straus has recently argued that the NVAW Survey generated annual rates of physical assault by an intimate partner that are substantially lower than those generated by the NFVS because the NVAW Survey was presented to respondents as a survey on personal safety.[19] According to Straus, the use of the term "personal safety" led many respondents to perceive of the NVAW Survey as a crime study and therefore to restrict their reports to "real crimes."

Aside from being inherently unconvincing—the terms "crime" and "personal safety" conjure up very different images—this theory fails to explain why the NVAW Survey generated high lifetime intimate partner victimization rates that are generally consistent with findings from other surveys or why the NVAW Survey uncovered high rates of other forms of family violence, such as incest and physical assault of children by adult caretakers (see chapter 6, "Violence Experienced as a Minor"). It is unlikely that using the term "personal safety" in the introduction of the NVAW Survey would have set up a perceptual screen for intimate partner violence experienced in the previous 12 months but not for intimate partner violence experienced over the course of the respondent's lifetime. Similarly, it is unlikely that using the term "personal safety" in the introduction of the NVAW Survey would have set up a perceptual screen for one type of family violence (e.g., physical assaults by marital/cohabiting partners) but not for other types of family violence (e.g., incest and physical assault by caretakers in childhood).

A more plausible explanation for the disparity in NFVS and NVAW Survey findings is the different ways the two surveys framed and introduced screening questions about intimate partner violence. In the NFVS, respondents are queried about specific acts of intimate partner violence they may have sustained or committed against their current partner. Published NFVS estimates of the number of women and men who experience intimate partner violence annually count both reports of perpetration and victimization. In other words, if a woman reported that she had committed an act of violence against her husband, her report was counted as a male victimization. To produce NFVS estimates that are directly comparable with NVAW Survey estimates, perpetrations reported to NFVS interviewers would have to be excluded. In addition, the NFVS introduces screening questions about intimate partner violence perpetration and victimization with an exculpatory statement that acknowledges the pervasiveness of marital/ partner conflict. Although this approach may seem more accepting of intimate partner violence and therefore more likely to result in disclosure of intimate partner violence, it may also be considered leading. Finally, the NFVS frames its screening questions in terms of *how many times in the past 12 months* respondents have committed or sustained these violent acts rather than *whether* they have ever perpetrated or sustained these violent acts. This approach assumes intimate partner violence is the norm and re-

quires respondents who neither committed nor sustained intimate partner violence in the past 12 months to provide an answer to the contrary.

By contrast, the NVAW Survey queries respondents only about their experiences with victimization, rather than victimization and perpetration. Further, the NVAW Survey does not use an exculpatory statement to introduce screening questions. And rather than asking respondents *how many times* they have sustained acts of intimate partner violence in the previous 12 months, the NVAW Survey asks respondents *whether* they ever sustained violent acts at the hands of any type of perpetrator, and if so, whether their perpetrator was a current or past intimate partner. Only respondents who report they have ever experienced such violent acts are asked whether these acts were perpetrated in the previous 12 months. Although this approach may be considered less accepting of intimate partner violence and therefore less likely to result in disclosure, it may also be considered less leading.

In summary, it is possible that the manner in which screening questions are introduced and framed has more of an effect on intimate partner violence disclosure rates than does the overall context in which the survey is administered. Clearly, more research is needed to fully understand how methodological factors (such as the overall context in which a survey is administered, question introduction, and framing practices) affect research findings on intimate partner violence. The need for this type of research was emphasized at the October 1998 workshop, "Building Data Systems for Monitoring and Responding to Violence Against Women," cosponsored by the U.S. Department of Health and Human Services and the U.S. Department of Justice.[20]

Notes

1. Straus, M.A., "Wifebeating: How Common and Why," *Victimology: An International Journal* 2 (3/4) (1977–78): 443–458.

2. See, for example, McNeely, R.L., and C.R. Mann, "Domestic Violence Is a Human Issue," *Journal of Interpersonal Violence* 5 (1990): 129–139; McNeely, R.L., and G. Robinson-Simpson, "The Truth About Domestic Violence: A Falsely Framed Issue," *Social Work* 32 (1987): 485–490; Shupe, A., W.A. Stacey, and L.R. Hazelwood, *Violent Men, Violent Couples: The Dynamics of Domestic Violence*, Lexington, MA: Lexington Books, 1987; Steinmetz, S.K., "The Battered Husband Syndrome," *Victimology: An International Journal* 2 (3/4) (1977–78): 499–509; Straus, M.A., "Physical Assault by Wives: A Major Social Problem," in *Current Controversies on Family Violence*, ed. R.J. Gelles and D.R. Loseke, Newbury Park, CA: Sage Publications, 1993: 67–87; Straus, M.A., and R.J. Gelles, "Societal Change and Change in Family Violence From 1975 to 1986 as Revealed by Two National Surveys," *Journal of Marriage and the Family* 48 (1986): 465–479.

3. See, for example, Berk, R.A., S.F. Berk, D.R. Loseke, and D. Rauma, "Mutual Combat and Other Family Victim Myths," in *The Dark Side of Families*, ed. D. Finkelhor, D.O. Gelles, G.T. Hotaling, and M.A. Straus, Beverly Hills, CA: Sage Publications, 1983: 197–212; Bograd, M., "Family Systems Approaches to Wife Battering: A Feminist Critique," *American Journal of Orthopsychiatry* 54 (1984): 558–568; Dobash, R.E., and R.P. Dobash, "Wives: The Appropriate Victims of Marital Violence," *Victimology: An International Journal* 2 (3/4) (1977–78): 426–443; Dobash, R.E., R.P. Dobash, M. Wilson, and M. Daly, "The Myth of Sexual Symmetry in Marital Violence," *Social Problems* 39 (1992): 71–91; Kurz, D., "Social Science Perspectives and Wife Abuse: Current Debates and Future Directions," *Gender and Society* 3 (1989): 501–513; Pleck, E., J.H. Pleck, M. Grossman, and P. Bart, "The Battered Date Syndrome: A Comment on Steinmetz's Article," *Victimology* 4 (1977–78): 131–140; Wardell, L., D.L. Gillespie, and A. Leffler, "Science and Violence Against Wives," in *The Dark Side of Families*, ed. D. Finkelhor, R.J. Gelles, G.T. Hotaling, and M.A. Straus, Beverly Hills, CA: Sage Publications, 1983: 69–84.

4. Russell, D.E.H., *Rape in Marriage*, Bloomington, IN: Indiana University Press, 1990.

5. Finkelhor, D., and K. Yllo, *License to Rape: Sexual Abuse of Wives*, New York: Holt, Rinehart and Winston, 1985.

6. Nisonoff, L., and I. Bittman, "Spouse Abuse: Incidence and Relationship to Selected Demographic Variables," *Victimology* 4 (1979): 131–140; Peterson, R., "Social Class, Social Learning, and Wife Abuse," *Social Service Review* 50 (1980): 390–406; Schulman, M., *A Survey of Spousal Violence Against Women in Kentucky*, Study Number 792701, Washington, DC: U.S. Department of Justice, Law Enforcement Assistance Administration, 1979; Teske, R.H.C., and M.L. Parker, *Spouse Abuse in Texas: A Study of Women's Attitudes and Experiences*, Newark, NJ: National Center for Crime and Delinquency, John Cotton Dana Library, 1983.

7. Ibid., Nisonoff and Bittman: "Spouse Abuse"; Scanzoni, J., *Sex Roles, Women's Work, and Marital Conflict*, Lexington, MA: Lexington Books, 1978.

8. Bureau of Justice Statistics, *Bureau of Justice Statistics Sourcebook of Criminal Justice Statistics— 1997*, Washington, DC: U.S. Department of Justice, Bureau of Justice Statistics, 1998, NCJ 171147: 198.

9. Bachman, R., and L.E. Saltzman, *Violence Against Women: Estimates From the Redesigned Survey*, Special Report, Washington, DC: U.S. Department of Justice, Bureau of Justice Statistics, 1995, NCJ 154348.

10. Greenfeld, L., M.R. Rand, D. Craven, P.A. Klaus, C.A. Perkins, C. Ringel, G. Warchol, C. Matson, and J.A. Fox, *Violence by Intimates: Analysis of Data on Crimes by Current or Former Spouses, Boyfriends, and Girlfriends*, Bureau of Justice Statistics Factbook, Washington, DC: U.S. Department of Justice, Bureau of Justice Statistics, 1998, NCJ 167237.

11. Straus and Gelles, "Societal Change and Change in Family Violence From 1975 to 1985 as Revealed by Two National Surveys" (see note 2, last entry).

12. Straus, M.A., "Trends in Cultural Norms and Rates of Partner Violence: An Update to 1992," in *Understanding Causes, Consequences, and Solutions*, Families in Focus Series, ed. M.A. Straus and S.M. Smith, Minneapolis: National Council on Family Relations, 1995: 30–33.

13. Schaefer, J., R. Caetano, and C.L. Clark, "Rates of Intimate Partner Violence in the United States," *American Journal of Public Health* 88 (11) (1998): 1702–1704.

14. Tjaden, P., and N. Thoennes, "Prevalence and Consequences of Male-to-Female and Female-to-Male Intimate Partner Violence as Measured by the National Violence Against Women Survey," *Violence Against Women* 6 (2) (2000): 142–161.

15. Straus and Gelles, "Societal Change and Change in Family Violence From 1975 to 1985 as Revealed by Two National Surveys" (see note 2, last entry).

16. Bachman, R., *Violence Against Women: A National Crime Victimization Survey Report*, Washington, DC: U.S. Department of Justice, Bureau of Justice Statistics, 1994, NCJ 145325; Bachman and Saltzman, *Violence Against Women: Estimates From the Redesigned Survey*, note 9; Gaquin, D., "Spouse Abuse: Data from the National Crime Survey," *Victimology* 2 (1977–78): 634–643; Klaus, P., and M. Rand, *Family Violence*, Special Report, Washington, DC: U.S. Department of Justice, Bureau of Justice Statistics, 1984, NCJ 093449.

17. See, for example, Klaus and Rand, *Family Violence* (see note 16, last entry); and Straus, M.A., "Physical Assault By Wives: A Major Social Problem" (see note 2).

18. Bachman, R., "A Comparison of Annual Incidence Rates and Contextual Characteristics of Intimate-Partner Violence Against Women from the National Crime Victimization Survey (NCVS) and the National Violence Against Women Survey (NVAWS)," *Violence Against Women* 6 (8) (August 2000): 839–867.

19. Straus, M.A., "The Controversy over Domestic Violence by Women: A Methodological, Theoretical, and Sociology of Science Analysis," in *Violence in Intimate Relationships*, ed. X.B. Arriaga and B. Oskamp, Thousand Oaks, CA: Sage Publications, 1999.

20. A report on the October 1998 workshop, "Building Data Systems for Monitoring and Responding to Violence Against Women," will be published by the Centers for Disease Control and Prevention (CDC) in the Recommendations and Reports series of the *Morbidity and Mortality Weekly Report (MMWR)*. The *MMWR* is available at the CDC Web site (http://www.cdc.gov/mmwr).

6. Violence Experienced as a Minor

This chapter focuses on violence women and men experienced as children and adolescents. It examines the extent to which women and men were raped and stalked before age 18 by all types of perpetrators and physically assaulted as children by adult caretakers. It also examines the relationship between victimization as a minor and subsequent victimization.

Prevalence of Violence in Childhood and Adolescence

Results from the NVAW Survey show that violence begins at an early age for many Americans. Nine percent of surveyed women and 1.9 percent of surveyed men said they were raped by any type of assailant before age 18. Forty percent of surveyed women and 53.8 percent of surveyed men said they experienced some type of physical assault by an adult caretaker as a child. In addition, 0.9 percent of surveyed women and 0.2 percent of surveyed men reported they were stalked by any type of perpetrator before age 18. Thus, about half of all respondents to the NVAW Survey (43.4 percent of the women and 54.3 percent of the men) experienced some type of violence as a child or adolescent (see exhibit 12). This figure probably underestimates the extent of violence experienced by respondents in childhood and adolescence because it excludes physical assaults they experienced before age 18 at the hands of strangers, acquaintances, intimates, and other relatives.

Rape Experienced as a Minor

It has been previously reported that rape in America is a "tragedy of youth" because the majority of rape victims are victimized before age 18.[1] Results from the NVAW Survey support this assertion: Of the respondents who reported *ever* being raped, 21.6 percent of the women and 48.0 percent of the men were younger than age 12 when they experienced their first rape, and 32.4 percent of the women and 23.0 percent of the men were ages 12–17. Thus, more than half (54 percent) of the female rape victims and nearly three-quarters (71 percent) of the male victims identified by the survey were younger than age 18 when they experienced their first attempted or completed rape (see exhibit 13).

Results from the NVAW Survey show that most children and adolescents are raped by someone they know. Only 14.3 percent of the women and 19.5 percent of the men raped before age 18 were raped by a stranger. In comparison, nearly

Exhibit 12. Persons Victimized Before Age 18 by Type of Victimization and Victim Gender		
Type of Victimization*	Women (%) (*n*=8,000)	Men (%) (*n*=8,000)
Rape	9.0	1.9
Physical assault by a caretaker	40.0	53.8
Stalking	0.9	0.2
Any of the above	43.4	54.3
*Differences between women and men are statistically significant for all types of victimization: χ^2, *p*-value $\leq$ .001.		

half of the women and men (46.7 and 44.2 percent, respectively) raped before age 18 were raped by an acquaintance; about one-third (38.8 and 30.5 percent, respectively) were raped by a relative other than a spouse; and 15 percent of the women and 6.5 percent of the men were raped by a current or former intimate partner (see exhibit 14).

Although rape is legally defined as a gender-neutral crime, females are the primary victims of rape occurring in childhood and adolescence, and males are the primary perpetrators. Surveyed women were nearly five times more likely

than surveyed men to report they had been raped as a child or adolescent. And the vast majority of women and men raped as children or adolescents (99.2 and 89.0 percent, respectively) were raped by a male. It is unclear from the survey data whether these male rapists were minors or adults.

Physical Assault by an Adult Caretaker

As the National Research Council has noted, assaults of children by their parents tend to go unrecognized because they are socially construed as discipline rather than violence, and

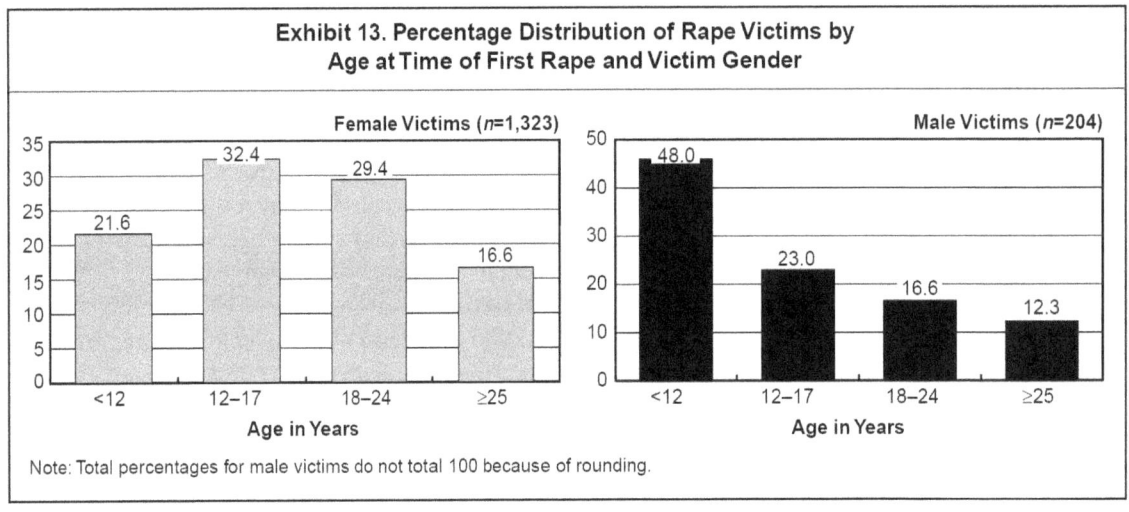

Exhibit 13. Percentage Distribution of Rape Victims by Age at Time of First Rape and Victim Gender

Female Victims (n=1,323)

Male Victims (n=204)

Note: Total percentages for male victims do not total 100 because of rounding.

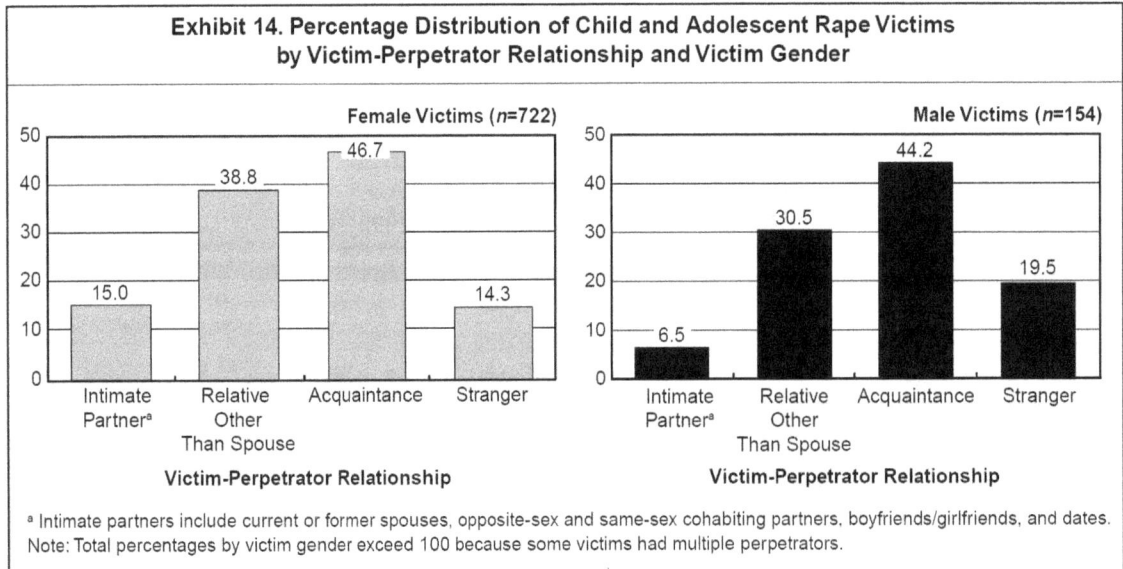

Exhibit 14. Percentage Distribution of Child and Adolescent Rape Victims by Victim-Perpetrator Relationship and Victim Gender

Female Victims (n=722)

Male Victims (n=154)

a Intimate partners include current or former spouses, opposite-sex and same-sex cohabiting partners, boyfriends/girlfriends, and dates.
Note: Total percentages by victim gender exceed 100 because some victims had multiple perpetrators.

current institutional systems for counting violent victimization in the United States are particularly problematic with respect to violence perpetrated against children by family members.[2] For example, the Bureau of Justice Statistics (BJS) National Crime Victimization Survey (NCVS) only interviews household members age 12 and older and allows parents to serve as proxy respondents for underage children. Thus, for an assault of a child by an adult caretaker to be counted by the NCVS, the victim would have to be age 12 or older, be interviewed by an NCVS interviewer, and overcome the fear and embarrassment associated with recounting the event to an interviewer. For such an assault to be counted in the Federal Bureau of Investigation (FBI) Uniform Crime Reports (UCR), the assault would require a report by a self-incriminating parent, a courageous victim or other family member, or an institutional official.[3] At present, the primary source of information about assaults perpetrated by parents against children is information generated by municipal, county, or State social service or child protective services agencies that investigate reports of suspected child maltreatment. School, social service, and medical professionals report such suspected child maltreatment based on physical evidence of possible physical harm they have observed. Unfortunately, even when such evidence is noted, the social service agency investigating the report may have no basis for determining whether the assault was inflicted by a parent.[4]

To generate information about the prevalence of physical assaults of children by their adult caretakers, respondents to the survey were asked a series of behaviorally specific questions about a range of physical assaults they may have experienced as children at the hands of parents, stepparents, or other adult caretakers. To ensure that these screening questions would elicit only a *yes* response to acts that constituted potential or actual violence rather than to accidental or unintentional acts such as being hit with a baseball during a game of catch, respondents

were told prior to being asked these questions that they were going to be asked questions about *violence* they experienced as children at the hands of adult caretakers (see "Survey Screening Questions" in chapter 2).

Nearly half of the respondents said they had experienced at least one physical assault by an adult caretaker as a child (see exhibit 15). Most of these assaults consisted of pushing, grabbing, shoving, slapping, hitting, and being hit with an object. Fewer respondents reported that an adult caretaker threw something at them that could hurt, kicked or bit them, pulled their hair, choked or tried to drown them, or beat them up. Only a negligible number reported an adult caretaker threatened them with a gun or knife or used a gun or knife on them.

It is unclear from the survey data how many of these physical assaults were executed in the context of the caretaker administering punishment to the respondent and were therefore socially defined as discipline rather than violence by the caretaker or child at the time of the assault. Because the screening questions were introduced as questions about violence experienced in childhood at the hands of adult caretakers, it can be assumed that respondents who disclosed this type of assault defined these acts as violence at the time of the interview.

Results from the survey show that boys are at significantly greater risk of physical assault by an adult caretaker than are girls. Compared with their female counterparts, surveyed men were significantly more likely to report that an adult caretaker threw something at them that could hurt; pushed, grabbed, or shoved them; slapped or hit them; kicked or bit them; hit them with an object; beat them up; or threatened them with a knife (exhibit 15).

The survey found that the prevalence of physical assault against children by adult caretakers has remained fairly stable over time. Women and men age 25 or younger at the time of the interview were just as likely to report being physically assaulted by an adult caretaker as women and men age 50 or older at the time of the interview.

Stalking Before Age 18

Results from the survey show that stalking is not a crime that is commonly perpetrated against minors. Less than 1 percent of women surveyed and 0.2 percent of men surveyed reported they were stalked before age 18 (exhibit 12). Among respondents who reported ever being stalked, 12.4 percent of the women and 9.5 percent of the men said they experienced their first stalking before age 18 (see exhibit 16).

Information from the survey shows that more than half (57.7 percent) of the women who were stalked

Exhibit 15. Persons Physically Assaulted as a Child by an Adult Caretaker by Type of Assault and Victim Gender		
Type of Assault	**Women (%)** **(*n*=8,000)**	**Men (%)** **(*n*=8,000)**
Total reporting physical assault by a caretaker[a]	**40.0**	**53.8**
Threw something that could hurt[a]	6.1	8.5
Pushed, grabbed, shoved[a]	15.8	25.4
Pulled hair	11.5	12.3
Slapped, hit[a]	33.5	44.1
Kicked, bit[a]	3.0	3.8
Choked, tried to drown	1.5	1.2
Hit with an object[a]	17.0	26.0
Beat up[b]	5.5	6.4
Threatened with a gun	0.9	0.8
Threatened with a knife[b]	1.4	2.1
Used a gun	0.4	0.4
Used a knife	1.1	1.3
[a]Differences between women and men are statistically significant: χ^2, *p*-value ≤ .001.		
[b]Differences between women and men are statistically significant: χ^2, *p*-value ≤ .05.		

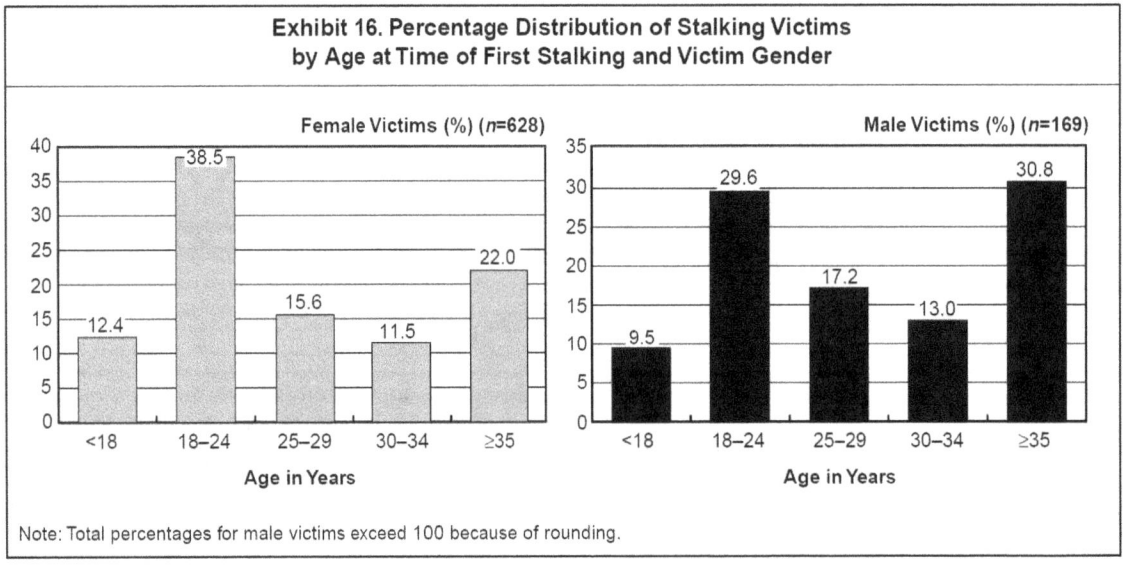

Exhibit 16. Percentage Distribution of Stalking Victims by Age at Time of First Stalking and Victim Gender

Note: Total percentages for male victims exceed 100 because of rounding.

Exhibit 19. Persons Physically Assaulted as an Adult by Whether They Were Physically Assaulted/Not Physically Assaulted as a Minor and Victim Gender				
	Women (%)*		Men (%)*	
Physically assaulted as an adult	Physically Assaulted as a Minor (*n*=3,198)	Not Physically Assaulted as a Minor (*n*=4,802)	Physically Assaulted as a Minor (*n*=4,307)	Not Physically Assaulted as a Minor (*n*=3,693)
Yes	46.7	19.8	60.0	27.3
No	53.3	80.2	40.0	72.7

*Differences between women and men who were "physically assaulted as a minor" and "not physically assaulted as a minor" are statistically significant: χ^2, *p*-value $\leq$ .001.

Exhibit 20. Women Stalked as an Adult by Whether They Were Stalked/Not Stalked as a Minor		
Stalked as an adult*	Stalked as a Minor (%) (*n*=73)	Not Stalked as a Minor (%) (*n*=7,927)
Yes	46.6	7.0
No	53.4	93.0

*Differences between women "stalked as a minor" and "not stalked as a minor" are statistically significant: χ^2, *p*-value $\leq$ .001.

reported being physically assaulted as an adult, only 19.8 percent of the women and 27.3 percent of the men who did not report being physically assaulted by an adult caretaker as a child did so. Thus, women and men who were physically assaulted by an adult caretaker as a child were twice as likely to be physically assaulted as an adult (see exhibit 19).

Finally, results from the survey indicate there is a relationship between being stalked as a minor and being stalked as an adult. Surveyed women who reported being stalked before age 18 were nearly seven times more likely to report being stalked since age 18 than women who were not stalked before age 18 (see exhibit 20). The number of male stalking victims was insufficient to analyze the relationship between victimization as a minor and subsequent victimization as an adult.

While these findings appear to show a strong relationship between victimization as a minor and subsequent victimization, they should be viewed with caution because they simply may reflect differences among respondents' willingness to disclose victimization rather than differences in actual victimization experiences. Respondents who felt comfortable disclosing violence they experienced as a minor may also have felt more comfortable disclosing violence they experienced as an adult, while respondents who felt uncomfortable disclosing violence experienced as a minor may also have felt uncomfortable disclosing violence experienced as an adult. Clearly, more research is needed on the relationship between victimization as a minor and subsequent adult victimization.

Notes

1. The National Women's Study found that 29 percent of forcible rapes of females occurred when the victim was younger than age 11, and 32 percent occurred when the victim was between ages 11 and 17. See National Victim Center and the Crime Victims Research and Treatment Center, *Rape in America: A Report to the Nation*, 211 Wilson Boulevard, Suite 200, Arlington, VA 22201, April 23, 1992: 15.

2. National Research Council, *Understanding and Preventing Violence*, Washington, DC: National Academy Press, 1993: 46–48.

3. Ibid.

4. Ibid.

5. See, for example, Browne, A., and D. Finkelhor, "Initial and Long-Term Effects: A Review of the Research," in *Source Book on Child Sexual Abuse*, ed. D. Finkelhor, Beverly Hills, CA: Sage Publications, 1986: 158; Miller, J., D. Moeller, A. Kaufman, P. Divasto, P. Fitzsimmons, D. Pather, and J. Christy, "Recidivism Among Sexual Assault Victims," *American Journal of Psychiatry* 135 (1978): 1103–1104; Russell, D.E.H., *The Secret Trauma: Incest in the Lives of Girls and Women*, New York: Basic Books, 1986.

7. Violence Experienced as an Adult

This chapter focuses on violence women and men experienced as adults. It examines the extent to which women and men were raped, physically assaulted, and/or stalked *since age 18* by all types of assailants.

Prevalence of Violence Experienced as an Adult

The NVAW Survey found that violence against adults is widespread. More than 1 in 3 surveyed women and nearly 1 in 2 surveyed men reported they were raped, physically assaulted, and/or stalked since age 18. Among surveyed women, the most frequently reported violence experienced as an adult was physical assault, followed by rape, and then stalking. For men, the most frequently reported violence experienced as an adult was physical assault, followed by stalking, and then rape (see exhibit 21).

Rape Experienced as an Adult

Nearly 10 percent of surveyed women, compared with less than 1 percent of surveyed men, reported being raped since age 18 (exhibit 21). Thus, U.S. women are 10 times more likely than U.S. men to be raped as an adult.

The survey found that most women who are raped as adults are raped by intimates. Nearly two-thirds (61.9 percent) of the women who reported being raped since age 18 were raped by a current or former spouse, cohabiting partner, boyfriend, or date. In comparison 21.3 percent were raped by an acquaintance, 16.7 were raped by a stranger, and 6.5 percent were raped by a relative (see exhibit 22). The number of male rape victims was insufficient to reliably calculate estimates for men.

Physical Assault Experienced as an Adult

About one-third (30.6 percent) of women surveyed and nearly half (44.9 percent) of men surveyed said they had been physically assaulted since age 18. Thus, U.S. men are 1.5 times more likely than U.S. women to be physically assaulted as an adult when all types of assaults and all types of assailants are considered.

The most frequently reported types of physical assault by both women and men were pushing, grabbing, shoving, slapping, and hitting. Although women were significantly more likely to report someone had pulled their hair, choked them, or tried to drown them since age 18, men were significantly more likely to report every other type of physical assault with one notable exception: Women and men were equally likely to report that they had been beaten since becoming an adult (see exhibit 23).

Results from the survey indicate that 1 of 9 Americans—female and male alike—has been beaten since age 18. Results also indicate that 1 of 18 U.S. women and 1 of 8 U.S. men has been threatened with a gun since becoming an adult, while 1 of 43 U.S. women and 1 of 20 U.S. men has had a gun used on them.

Exhibit 21. Persons Victimized Since Age 18 by Type of Victimization and Victim Gender		
Type of Victimization*	Women (%) (*n*=8,000)	Men (%) (*n*=8,000)
Rape	9.6	0.8
Physical assault	30.6	44.9
Rape and/or physical assault	33.4	45.1
Stalking	7.4	2.1
Any of the above	38.8	46.1
*Differences between women and men are statistically significant: χ^2, *p*-value ≤ .001.		

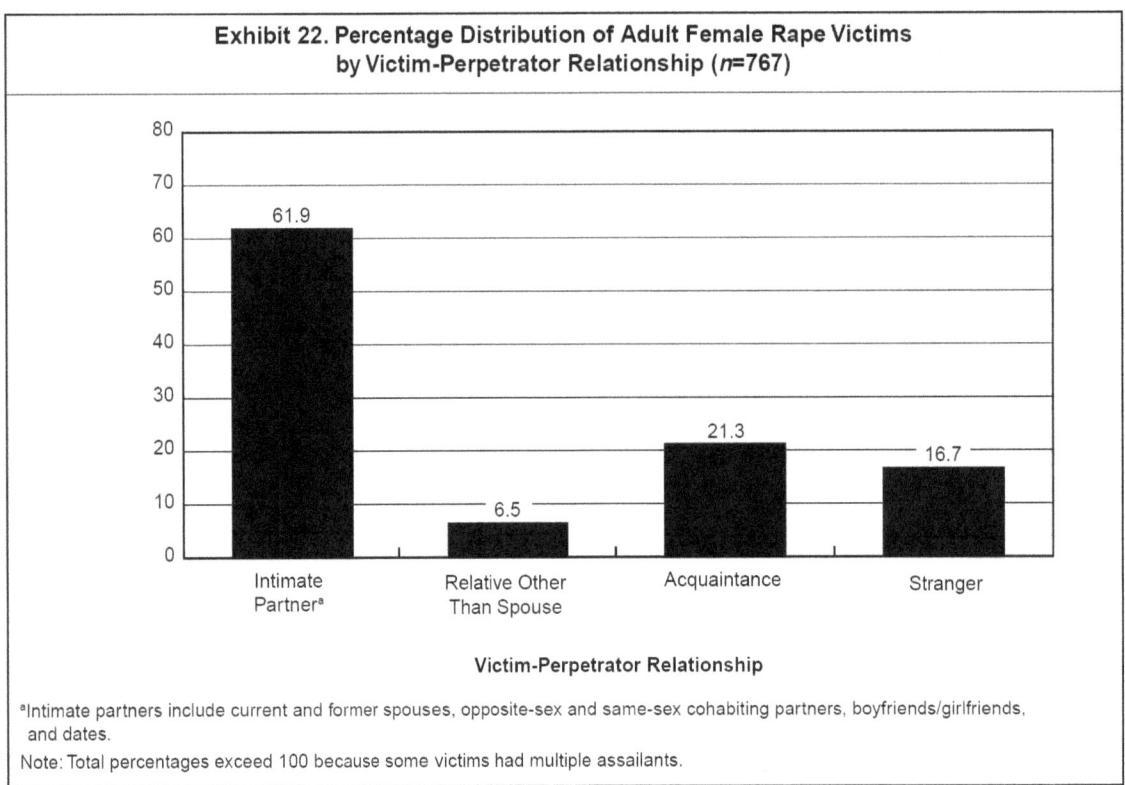

Exhibit 22. Percentage Distribution of Adult Female Rape Victims by Victim-Perpetrator Relationship (*n*=767)

Intimate Partner[a]	61.9
Relative Other Than Spouse	6.5
Acquaintance	21.3
Stranger	16.7

Victim-Perpetrator Relationship

[a]Intimate partners include current and former spouses, opposite-sex and same-sex cohabiting partners, boyfriends/girlfriends, and dates.

Note: Total percentages exceed 100 because some victims had multiple assailants.

Exhibit 23. Persons Physically Assaulted Since Age 18 by Type of Assault and Victim Gender

Type of Assault*	Women (%) (*n*=8,000)	Men (%) (*n*=8,000)
Total reporting physical assault since age 18	**30.6**	**44.9**
Threw something that could hurt	10.3	17.8
Pushed, grabbed, shoved	23.3	32.9
Pulled hair	11.4	8.7
Slapped, hit	21.1	28.2
Kicked, bit	6.9	12.7
Choked, tried to drown	6.8	3.0
Hit with an object	7.4	15.9
Beat up	10.7	10.9
Threatened with a gun	5.5	12.7
Threatened with a knife	4.8	15.1
Used gun	2.3	4.9
Used knife	2.7	8.9

*With the exception of "beat up," differences between women and men are statistically significant: χ^2, *p*-value $\leq$ .001.

It has been previously reported that U.S. women are most frequently assaulted by intimate partners.[1] Information from the survey supports this assertion. Nearly three-quarters (72.1 percent) of the women who reported being physically assaulted as an adult were assaulted by a current or former husband, cohabiting partner, boyfriend, or date; 11.5 percent were assaulted by an acquaintance; 10.6 percent were assaulted by a stranger; and 7.0 percent were assaulted by a relative other than a spouse (see exhibit 24).

In comparison, results from the NVAW Survey show that U.S. men are at greatest risk of being physically assaulted by a stranger. More than half (56.2 percent) of the men who reported being physically assaulted since age 18 were assaulted by a stranger; 29.9 percent were assaulted by an acquaintance; 16.6 percent were assaulted by a current or former wife, cohabiting partner, girlfriend, or date; and 6.3 percent were assaulted by a relative other than a spouse (exhibit 24).

Stalking Experienced as an Adult

The survey found that 7.4 percent of surveyed women and 2.1 percent of surveyed men reported being stalked since age 18 (exhibit 21). Thus,

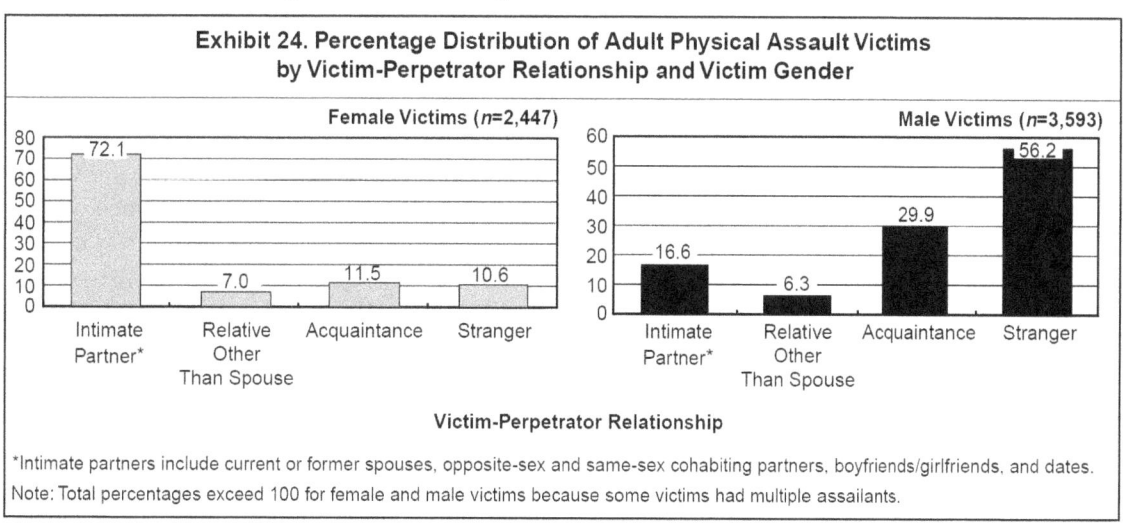

Exhibit 24. Percentage Distribution of Adult Physical Assault Victims by Victim-Perpetrator Relationship and Victim Gender

*Intimate partners include current or former spouses, opposite-sex and same-sex cohabiting partners, boyfriends/girlfriends, and dates.

Note: Total percentages exceed 100 for female and male victims because some victims had multiple assailants.

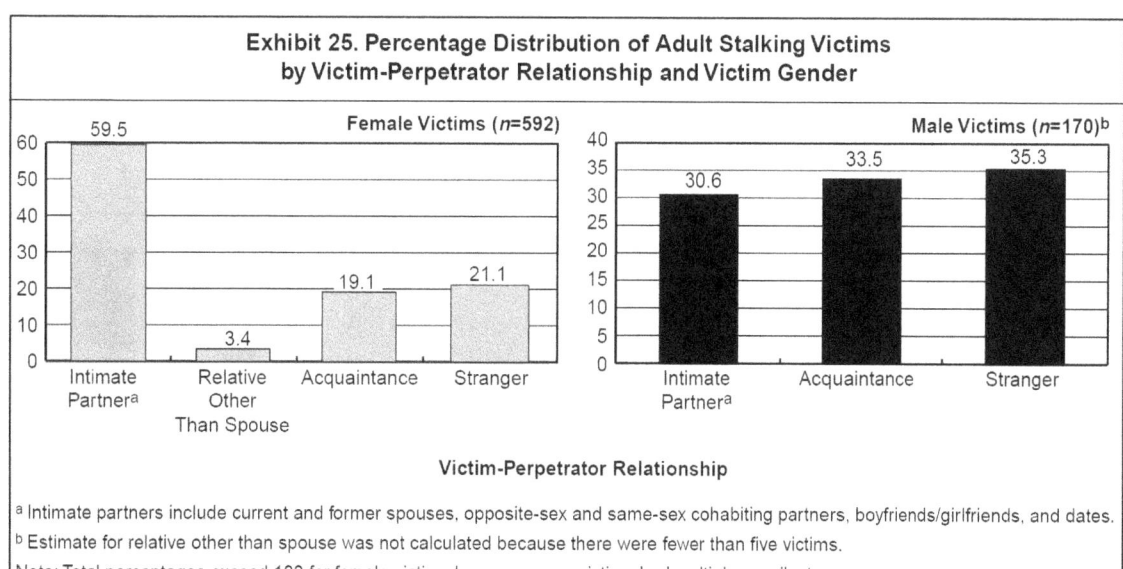

Exhibit 25. Percentage Distribution of Adult Stalking Victims by Victim-Perpetrator Relationship and Victim Gender

a Intimate partners include current and former spouses, opposite-sex and same-sex cohabiting partners, boyfriends/girlfriends, and dates.

b Estimate for relative other than spouse was not calculated because there were fewer than five victims.

Note: Total percentages exceed 100 for female victims because some victims had multiple assailants.

U.S. women are nearly four times more likely than U.S. men to be stalked as an adult.

The survey confirms previous reports that most victims know their stalker.[2] Among respondents who were stalked as adults, about one-fifth (21.1 percent) of the women and one-third (35.3 percent) of the men were stalked by a stranger. Typically, women are stalked by current or former intimates, while men are nearly equally likely to be stalked by current and former intimates, acquaintances, and strangers. Very few women and men are stalked by a relative other than a spouse (see exhibit 25).

Violence Against Women Is Predominantly Intimate Partner Violence

Results from the survey confirm previous reports that violence against women is predominantly intimate partner violence:[3] 64.0 percent of the women who were raped, physically assaulted, and/or stalked since age 18 were victimized by a current or former husband, cohabiting partner, boyfriend, or date; 16.4 percent were victimized by an acquaintance; 14.6 percent were victimized by a stranger; and 6.4 percent were victimized by a relative other than a husband (see exhibit 26).

In comparison, results from the survey indicate U.S. men are predominantly victimized by strangers: 50.4 percent of the men who reported being raped, physically assaulted, and/or stalked since age 18 were victimized by a stranger; 27.2 percent were victimized by an acquaintance; 16.2 percent were victimized by a current or former wife, cohabiting partner, girlfriend, or date; and 4.2 percent were victimized by a relative other than a wife (exhibit 26).

When only victims of rape and/or physical assault are considered, the results are similar: Women are predominantly victimized by current and former intimate partners and men are predominantly victimized by strangers (see exhibit 27).

Violence Against Women and Men Is Predominantly Male Violence

Results from the survey show that violence against women is predominantly male violence: All women who were raped since age 18 were raped by a male. (The number of women who were raped by a female since age 18 was too small (<5) to reliably calculate estimates.) The vast majority (91.9 percent) of women who were physically assaulted since age 18 were assaulted by a male, while only 11.8 percent were physically assaulted by a female. And nearly all (97.2 percent) women who were stalked since age 18 were stalked by a male (see exhibit 28). (The number of women who were stalked by a female since age 18 was too small (<5) to reliably calculate estimates.)

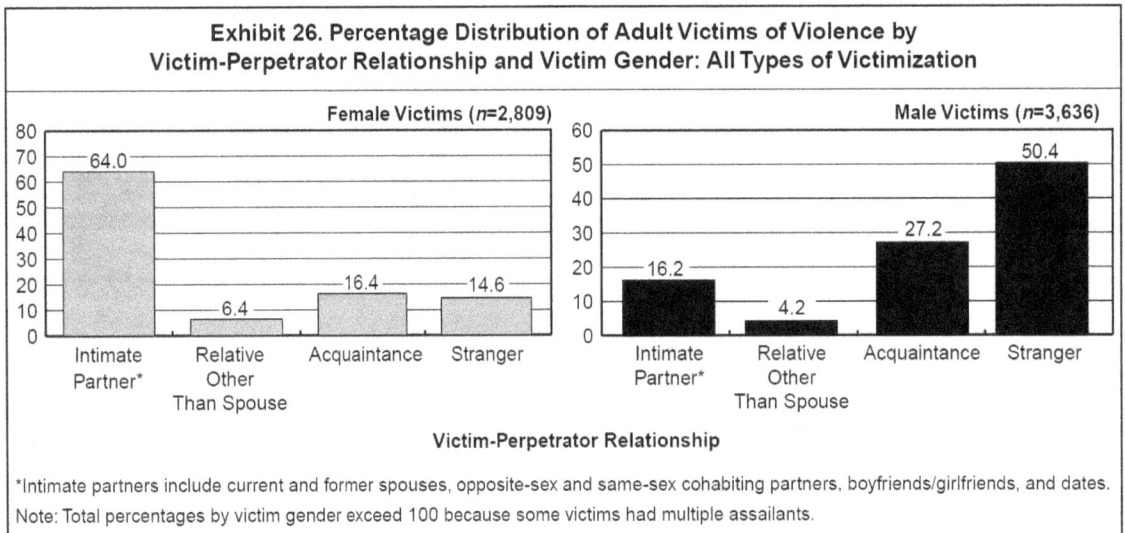

Exhibit 26. Percentage Distribution of Adult Victims of Violence by Victim-Perpetrator Relationship and Victim Gender: All Types of Victimization

*Intimate partners include current and former spouses, opposite-sex and same-sex cohabiting partners, boyfriends/girlfriends, and dates.

Note: Total percentages by victim gender exceed 100 because some victims had multiple assailants.

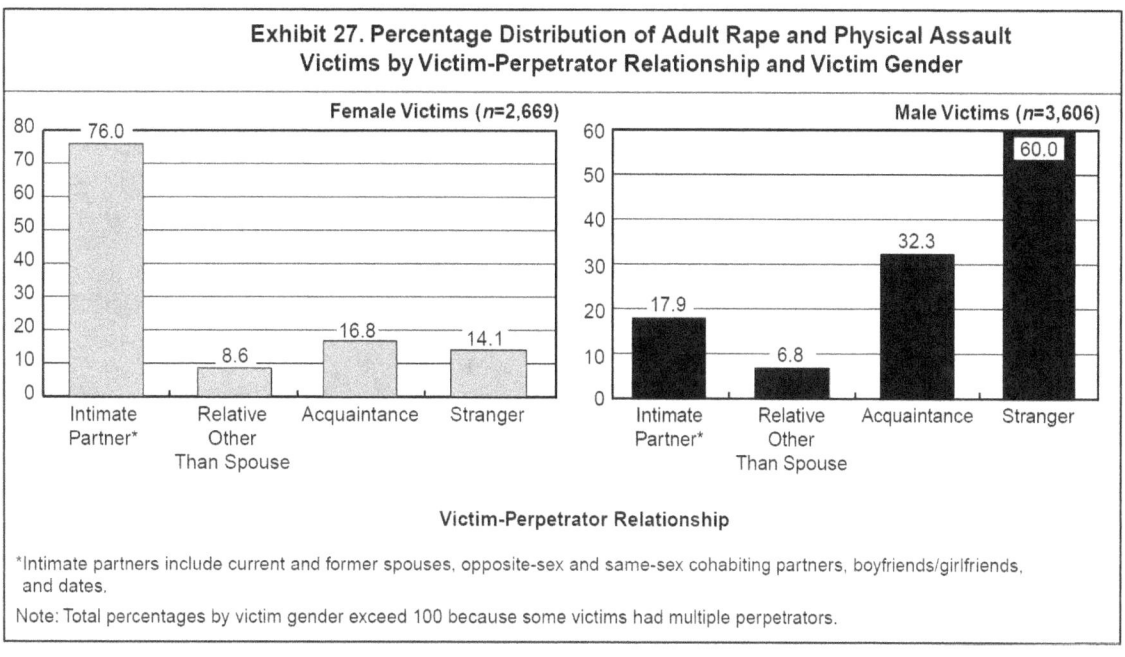

Exhibit 27. Percentage Distribution of Adult Rape and Physical Assault Victims by Victim-Perpetrator Relationship and Victim Gender

*Intimate partners include current and former spouses, opposite-sex and same-sex cohabiting partners, boyfriends/girlfriends, and dates.

Note: Total percentages by victim gender exceed 100 because some victims had multiple perpetrators.

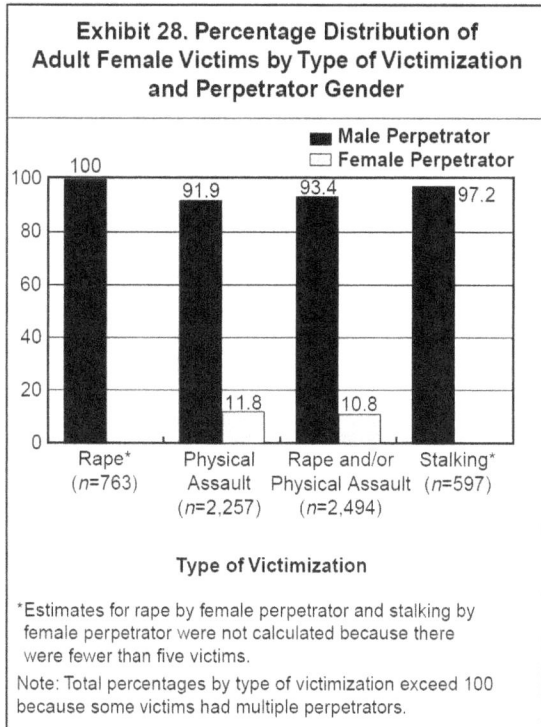

Exhibit 28. Percentage Distribution of Adult Female Victims by Type of Victimization and Perpetrator Gender

*Estimates for rape by female perpetrator and stalking by female perpetrator were not calculated because there were fewer than five victims.

Note: Total percentages by type of victimization exceed 100 because some victims had multiple perpetrators.

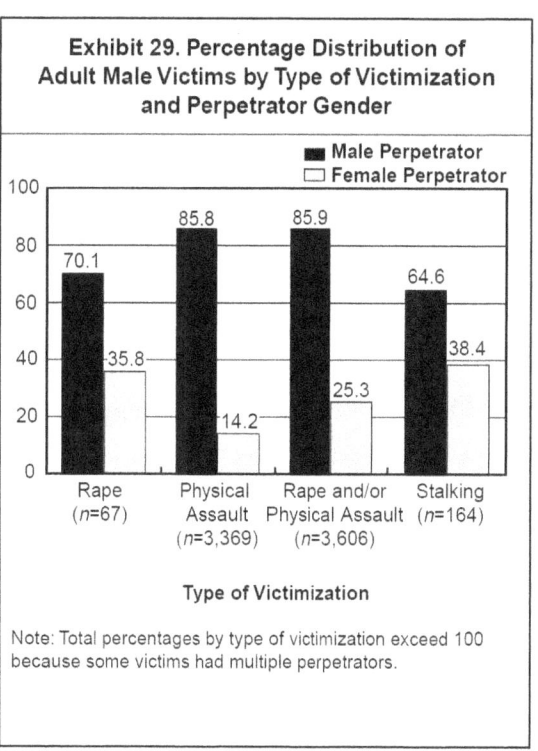

Exhibit 29. Percentage Distribution of Adult Male Victims by Type of Victimization and Perpetrator Gender

Note: Total percentages by type of victimization exceed 100 because some victims had multiple perpetrators.

Information from the survey shows that violence against men is also predominantly male violence: Most (70.1 percent) men who were raped since age 18 were raped by a male, while 35.8 percent were raped by a female. Similarly, most (85.8 percent) men who were physically assaulted since age 18 were physically assaulted by a man, while only 14.2 percent were physically assaulted by a woman. Finally, nearly two-thirds (64.6 percent) of the men who were stalked since age 18 were stalked by a male, while 38.4 percent were stalked by a female (see exhibit 29).

Notes

1. See National Research Council, *Understanding Violence Against Women*, Washington, DC: National Academy Press, 1996: 29–34.

2. A survey of 90 Florida law enforcement agencies reported that in most stalking cases the victim knew the offender. See Tucker, J.T., "The Effectiveness of Florida Stalking Statutes Section 784,048," *Florida Law Review* 45 (4) (1993): 609–707.

3. See, for example, Bachman, R., *Violence Against Women: A National Crime Victimization Survey Report*, Washington, DC: U.S. Department of Justice, Bureau of Justice Statistics, 1994, NCJ 145325; Bachman, R., and L.E. Saltzman, *Violence Against Women: Estimates From the Redesigned Survey*, Special Report, Washington, DC: U.S. Department of Justice, Bureau of Justice Statistics, 1995, NCJ 154348; Gaquin, D., "Spouse Abuse: Data from the National Crime Survey," *Victimology* 2 (1977–78): 634–643; Klaus, P., and M. Rand, *Family Violence*, Special Report, Washington, DC: U.S. Department of Justice, Bureau of Justice Statistics, 1984, NCJ 093449.

8. Physical Injury and Use of Medical Services

To generate information on violence-related injuries, survey respondents who reported being raped or physically assaulted were asked whether they were injured during their most recent victimization by each perpetrator they identified. Victims disclosing they were injured were asked to describe the nature of their injuries and whether they sought medical treatment for them.

This chapter examines the injury rate among rape and physical assault victims and the frequency with which they obtained specific types of medical treatment for their injuries. Also included in this chapter are estimates of the number of rapes and physical assaults that result in injury and the use of medical services annually. The injury and medical utilization estimates presented are based on information gathered on the most recent rape and physical assault experienced by victims *since age 18.* For some victims this incident happened in the past year; for others it happened 10 or more years ago. About half of the rapes and physical assaults included in the analysis occurred within the past 5 years.

Rates of Injury Among Rape and Physical Assault Victims

The survey found that women who were raped since age 18 were nearly twice as likely as their male counterparts to report they sustained an injury other than the rape itself during their most recent victimization (31.5 and 16.1 percent, respectively) (see exhibit 30). Similarly, women who were physically assaulted since age 18 were significantly more likely than their male counterparts to report they were injured during their most recent physical assault (39.0 and 24.8 percent, respectively). When only physical assaults *by intimates* are considered, the difference between injury rates for women and men is even greater: 41.5 percent of the women and 19.9 percent of the men who were physically assaulted by an intimate since age 18 were injured during their most recent victimization.[1]

Most of the female and male rape and physical assault victims who reported being injured sustained relatively minor injuries, such as scratches, bruises, and welts. Relatively few

	Rape Victims (%)[b]		Physical Assault Victims (%)[b]	
Exhibit 30. Percentage Distribution of Adult Rape and Physical Assault Victims by Whether Victim Was Injured and Victim Gender[a]				
	Women (*n*=734)	Men (*n*=62)	Women (*n*=1,862)	Men (*n*=2,972)
Was victim injured?				
Yes	31.5	16.1	39.0	24.8
No	68.5	83.9	61.0	75.2

[a]Estimates are based on the most recent victimization since age 18.
[b]Differences between women and men are statistically significant: χ^2, *p*-value $\leq$ .001.

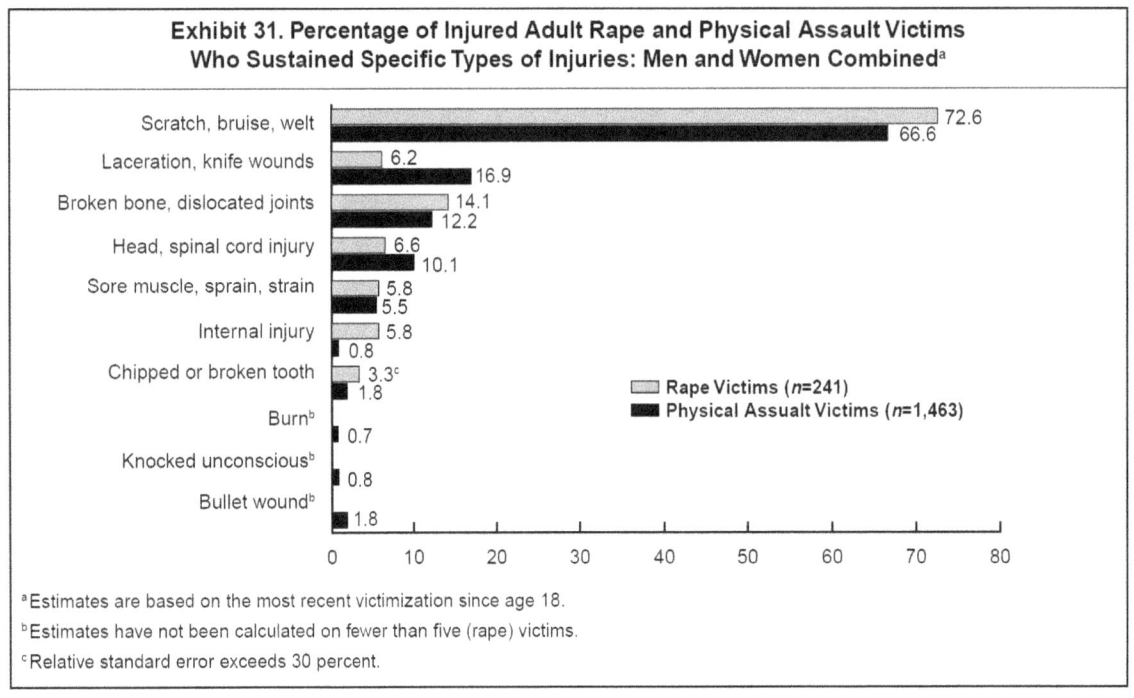

Exhibit 31. Percentage of Injured Adult Rape and Physical Assault Victims Who Sustained Specific Types of Injuries: Men and Women Combined[a]

Injury type	Rape Victims (n=241)	Physical Assault Victims (n=1,463)
Scratch, bruise, welt	72.6	66.6
Laceration, knife wounds	6.2	16.9
Broken bone, dislocated joints	14.1	12.2
Head, spinal cord injury	6.6	10.1
Sore muscle, sprain, strain	5.8	5.5
Internal injury	5.8	0.8
Chipped or broken tooth	3.3[c]	1.8
Burn[b]		0.7
Knocked unconscious[b]		0.8
Bullet wound[b]		1.8

[a] Estimates are based on the most recent victimization since age 18.
[b] Estimates have not been calculated on fewer than five (rape) victims.
[c] Relative standard error exceeds 30 percent.

sustained more serious types of injuries, such as broken bones, dislocated joints, concussions, lacerations, or bullet wounds (see exhibit 31).

Risk Factors Associated With Violence-Related Injury

Results of bivariable analyses

To identify characteristics of the victim, perpetrator, and incident that increase the risk of injury to rape and physical assault victims, a series of bivariable analyses were conducted that compared rates of injury for victims with and without select characteristics. The specific characteristics included in the bivariable analyses were:

- Whether the victim was white or nonwhite.

- Whether the victim was younger than 30 years of age or 30 years or older.

- Whether the incident occurred in the victim's or perpetrator's home or another location.

- Whether the perpetrator was a current or former intimate partner or a nonintimate.

- Whether the perpetrator threatened to harm or kill the victim or someone close to the victim.

- Whether the perpetrator used a weapon.

- Whether the perpetrator used drugs and/or alcohol at the time of the incident.

- Whether the victim used drugs and/or alcohol at the time of the incident.

- [*Rape victims only*] Whether the rape was completed or attempted.

In each bivariable analysis, the dependent variable was whether the victim was injured during his or her most recent victimization since the age of 18.

Results of the bivariable analyses show that risk of injury *increased* for female rape victims if the perpetrator was a current or former intimate partner, if the rape occurred in the victim's or perpetrator's home, if the rape was completed, if the perpetrator threatened to harm or kill the victim or someone close to the victim, if the perpetrator used a weapon, and if the perpetrator used drugs and/or alcohol at the time of the rape. Risk of injury for female rape victims *decreased* if the victim used drugs and/or alcohol at the time of the incident. No relationship was found between risk of injury for female rape victims and the victim's age or race (see exhibit 32).

	Rape Victims[b]		Physical Assault Victims			
	Women		Women		Men	
Characteristic	%	n	%	n	%	n
Total reporting injury	**31.5**	**(734)**	**39.0**	**(1,862)**	**24.8**	**(2,972)**
Victim's race						
White	31.1	(585)	39.0	(1,432)	24.7	(2,387)
Nonwhite	32.6	(141)	39.2	(395)	23.8	(512)
Victim's age						
Less than 30	30.7	(525)	38.0	(1,089)	25.8	(1,845)
30 and older	33.5	(209)	40.5	(773)	23.1	(1,127)
Incident location						
Home of victim/perpetrator	35.0[c]	(472)	40.2	(1,403)	21.3[d]	(747)
Location other than home	26.1	(241)	35.5	(459)	25.9	(2,225)
Rape outcome						
Completed	38.4[d]	(450)	NA		NA	
Attempted	20.3	(276)				
Victim-perpetrator relationship						
Intimate	36.2[c]	(459)	41.5[d]	(825)	19.9[d]	(488)
Nonintimate	23.6	(275)	31.3	(308)	26.0	(2,484)
Perpetrator threatened to harm or kill victim						
Threat	54.3[c]	(230)	53.5[d]	(600)	27.3[d]	(1,297)
No threat	21.0	(491)	32.0	(1,221)	22.4	(1,601)
Perpetrator used a weapon						
Weapon	57.0[c]	(79)	42.2	(296)	27.6[c]	(895)
No weapon	28.0	(692)	38.4	(1,562)	23.6	(2,059)
Perpetrator used drugs and/or alcohol						
Used	36.9[c]	(417)	46.0[d]	(923)	29.0[d]	(1,461)
Did not use	20.2	(208)	32.0	(709)	18.0	(844)
Victim used drugs and/or alcohol						
Used	25.0[d]	(144)	44.9[c]	(205)	33.1[d]	(953)
Did not use	33.4	(578)	38.3	(1,641)	21.9	(1,970)

Exhibit 32. Rape and Physical Assault Victims Who Were Injured by Characteristics of the Victimization and Victim Gender[a]

[a]Estimates are based on the most recent victimization since the age of 18.
[b]The number of male rape victims was insufficient to reliably calculate estimates.
[c]Differences between victims with and without characteristic are statistically significant: χ^2, p-value $\leq$ .05.
[d]Differences between victims with and without characteristic are statistically significant: χ^2, p-value $\leq$ .001.
Note: Numbers in parentheses indicate the size of the subgroup being analyzed. For example, the figure "(585)" in the row labeled "Victim's race—White" indicates there were 585 white female rape victims. The point estimate "31.1" next to this figure indicates that 31.1 percent of white female rape victims were injured during their most recent rape since the age of 18.

Results of the bivariable analyses also show that injury risk factors for female physical assault victims were somewhat similar to those for female rape victims in that risk of injury *increased* if the perpetrator was a current or former intimate partner, if the perpetrator threatened to harm or kill them or someone close to them, and if the perpetrator used drugs and/or alcohol at the time of the incident. However, injury risk factors for female physical assault victims were different from those for female rape victims in that risk of injury *increased* if the victim used drugs and/or alcohol at the time of the incident. No relationship was found between risk of injury for female physical assault victims and the location of the assault or the victim's age or race (exhibit 32).

Finally, results of the bivariable analyses for male physical assault victims show that the risk of injury *decreased* if the perpetrator was a current or former intimate partner. Conversely, the risk of injury *increased* if the perpetrator threatened to harm or kill them or someone close to them, if the perpetrator used a weapon, if the perpetrator used drugs and/or alcohol at the time of the incident, and if the victim used drugs and/or alcohol at the time of the incident. No relationship was found between risk of injury for male physical assault victims and the location of the incident or the victim's age or race (exhibit 32).

Results of multivariable analyses

Following the bivariable analyses, a series of logistic regressions were conducted using a backward stepwise procedure in which the independent variables that were found to be associated with victim injury in a series of bivariable analyses (exhibit 32) were regressed against a dependent variable representing victim injury. Separate analyses were conducted for women who reported being raped since the age of 18 (n = 600), women who reported being physically assaulted since the age of 18 (n = 1,589), and men who reported being physically assaulted since the age of 18 (n = 2,241). The goals of the multivariable analyses were to provide a measure by which the relative importance of the independent variables could be assessed and to determine which variables increased the odds that a victim would be injured. Logistic regression was used because of the dichotomous and unevenly distributed nature of the dependent variables. In order to check for multicollinearity among the independent variables, each variable's tolerance level was calculated using linear regression. Because none of the variables had a

tolerance of less than 0.600 (see sidebar "Results of the Logistic Regressions" in this chapter), multicollinearity was not considered a problem.

Injury risk factors during rape. Results of the logistic regression indicate that women who were raped as adults were significantly more likely to incur an injury (other than the rape itself) if they were raped by a current or former intimate partner; if their perpetrator threatened to harm or kill them or someone close to them at the time of the rape; if their perpetrator used a gun, knife, or other weapon during the rape; if the rape was completed; and if their perpetrator used drugs and/or alcohol at the time of the rape. The variable most likely to predict injury among adult female rape victims was whether the perpetrator threatened to harm or kill the victim or someone close to the victim at the time of the rape. Results of the logistic regression did not show a relationship between victim injury and the location of the rape or the victim's use of drugs and/or alcohol at the time of the rape (sidebar "Results of the Logistic Regressions").

Injury risk factors during physical assault. Results of the logistic regression show that female physical assault victims were more likely to be injured if they were assaulted by a current or former intimate partner, if their perpetrator threatened to harm or kill them or someone close to them at the time of the assault, and if their perpetrator used drugs and/or alcohol at the time of the assault (sidebar "Results of the Logistic Regressions"). The variable most likely to increase the risk of injury among female physical assault victims was whether their perpetrator threatened to harm or kill them or someone close to them at the time of the assault. Three variables did *not* predict whether a female physical assault victim was injured: the location of the assault, whether the perpetrator used a weapon, and whether the victim used drugs and/or alcohol.

Results of the logistic regression for male physical assault victims revealed somewhat different injury risk factors. Like their female counterparts, male physical assault victims were significantly more likely to be injured if their perpetrator threatened to harm or kill them or someone close to them and if their perpetrator used drugs and/or alcohol at the time of the incident. Unlike female victims, male victims using drugs and/or alcohol at the time of the physical assault were also significantly more likely to be injured (sidebar "Results of the Logistic Regressions").

Results of the Logistic Regressions

I. Model of the Relationship Between Independent Variables and Risk of Injury for Female Rape Victims

Variable	B	S.E.	Exp(b)	Tolerance
Perpetrator was an intimate*	.7881	.2238	2.1993	.907
Perpetrator threatened to harm or kill*	1.2773	.2086	3.5869	.840
Perpetrator used a weapon**	.8315	.3308	2.2966	.870
Rape was completed*	.6924	.2159	1.9986	.926
Perpetrator used drugs/alcohol**	.5955	.2190	1.8139	.819
Constant*	-2.7484	.2916		

χ^2=110.158 (p-value $\leq$ .0000) d.f.=5, n=600 *p-value $\leq$ .001 **p-value $\leq$ .01

II. Model of the Relationship Between Independent Variables and Risk of Injury for Female Physical Assault Victims

Variable	B	S.E.	Exp(b)	Tolerance
Perpetrator was an intimate**	.4170	.1400	1.5174	.817
Perpetrator threatened to harm or kill*	.9034	.1124	2.4680	.870
Perpetrator used drugs/alcohol*	.4841	.1089	1.6227	.901
Constant*	-1.3406	.1470		

χ^2=107.806 (p-value $\leq$ .0000) d.f.=3, n=1,589 *p-value $\leq$ .001 **p-value $\leq$ .01

III. Model of the Relationship Between Independent Variables and Risk of Injury for Male Physical Assault Victims

Variable	B	S.E.	Exp(b)	Tolerance
Perpetrator threatened to harm or kill***	.2267	.1092	1.2544	.814
Perpetrator used a weapon***	.2342	.1179	1.2639	.853
Victim used drugs/alcohol*	.4683	.1125	1.5973	.766
Perpetrator used drugs/alcohol**	.3346	.1239	1.3974	.695
Constant*	-1.6745	.0995		

χ^2=60.192 (p-value $\leq$ .0000) d.f.=4, n=2,241 *p-value $\leq$ .001 **p-value $\leq$ .01 ***p-value $\leq$ .05

Note: The chi-square statistic (χ^2) provides an indication of the overall fit of the data to the model. A significant chi-square indicates that the variables, as a group, contribute significantly to predicting the dependent variable (risk of injury) when compared with a model containing just the intercept. The logistic coefficients (B) and their standard errors (S.E.) can be interpreted as the change associated with a unit change in the explanatory variable when all other variables in the model are held constant. The logistic coefficients can be understood more easily if quoted as an odds ratio. The odds ratio [Exp (b)] provides the ratio of the odds of the p (the probability of an event happening) in the group responding yes to the explanatory variable relative to the group responding no to the explanatory variable while all other variables are held constant. For example, an odds ratio of 1 indicates changes in the explanatory variable do not lead to changes in the odds of p; a ratio of less than 1 indicates the odds of p decrease as x increases; and a ratio of greater than 1 indicates the odds of p increase as x increases. Variables are considered significant if they have a p-value of $\leq$ .05. Finally, each variable's tolerance is reported. This is a statistic that tests for multicollinearity among the independent variables in a model. Tolerances of more than 0.600 indicate no serious problem of collinearity.

Medical Care	Rape Victims (%)[b]	Physical Assault Victims (%)	
	Women	Women	Men
Did injured victim receive medical care?[c]	**(n=236)**	**(n=722)**	**(n=736)**
Yes	35.6	30.2	37.1
No	64.4	69.8	62.9
Type of medical care received[d]	**(n=84)**	**(n=218)**	**(n=306)**
Hospital care	81.9	76.1	85.7
Physician care	54.8	52.8	42.1
Dental care	16.9	9.6	10.6
Ambulance/paramedic care	19.0	17.5	23.5
Physical therapy	16.7	9.2	12.8
Type of hospital care received[e]	**(n=68)**	**(n=166)**	**(n=234)**
Emergency room	50.0	61.4	66.7
Outpatient	36.8	22.3	22.6
Inpatient	13.2[f]	15.1	10.3

Exhibit 33. Percentage Distribution of Injured Rape and Physical Assault Victims by Type of Medical Care Received and Victim Gender[a]

[a]Estimates are based on the most recent victimization since age 18.
[b]The number of male rape victims was insufficient to reliably calculate medical utilization estimates.
[c]Estimates are based on responses from victims who were injured.
[d]Estimates are based on responses from victims who received medical care.
[e]Estimates are based on responses from victims who received hospital care.
[f]Relative standard error exceeds 30 percent.
Note: Total percentages for type of medical and hospital care received exceed 100 because some victims had multiple forms of medical/hospital care.

In summary, results of the logistic regressions show a strong link between threats of bodily injury and actual occurrences of injury, regardless of the type of violence being perpetrated or the victim's gender. These findings suggest that threats of violence should be taken seriously and violence prevention strategies for both women and men should emphasize this fact. Results also show a strong link between victim injury and drug and alcohol use by the perpetrator. These findings suggest that some of the inhibitors that may prevent persons from hurting others under ordinary circumstances are relaxed when persons are under the influence of drugs and alcohol.

Injured Victims' Use of Medical Services

The survey found that about one-third (35.6 percent) of the women injured during their most recent rape since age 18 received some type of medical care (e.g., ambulance/paramedic services, hospitalization, and physical therapy) (see exhibit 33). (The number of male rape victims was insufficient to reliably calculate medical utilization estimates for men.) By far the most frequently reported medical treatment received for a rape injury was hospitalization: 81.9 percent of the women who received medical treatment as a result of their most recent rape were treated in a hospital. Of these women, half were treated in a hospital emergency department, 36.8 percent received other outpatient services and 13.2 percent spent at least one night in the hospital on an inpatient basis. More than half (54.8 percent) of the female rape victims who received medical care saw a physician outside of a hospital setting, and less than one-fifth received dental care (16.9 percent), ambulance or paramedic care (19.0 percent), or physical therapy (16.7 percent) (exhibit 33).

Exhibit 34. Average Number of Medical Care Visits for Rape and Physical Assault Victims by Type of Medical Care and Victim Gender[a]			
	Rape Victims[b]	Physical Assault Victims	
Type of Medical Care	Women[c]	Women[d]	Men[e]
Emergency room visit	3.2[f]	1.7	1.4
Outpatient visit	2.2	5.0[f]	2.8
Overnight in hospital	3.6	8.5[f]	13.3
Physician visit	4.8	3.3	7.2
Dental visit	5.0[f]	3.8	5.7
Ambulance/paramedic care	1.2	1.1	1.0
Physical therapy visit	13.0[f]	18.5[f]	10.8

[a]Estimates are based on the most recent victimization since age 18.

[b]The number of male rape victims was insufficient to reliably calculate medical utilization estimates.

[c]The standard error of the mean for each estimate in this column is 1.5, 0.4, 1.0, 0.9, 2.0, 0.1, and 4.3, respectively.

[d]The standard error of the mean for each estimate in this column is 0.2, 2.0, 3.4, 0.5, 1.0, 0.1, and 7.6, respectively.

[e]The standard error of the mean for each estimate in this column is 0.1, 0.8, 3.0, 1.3, 1.6, 0.02, and 2.5, respectively.

[f]Relative standard error exceeds 30 percent.

Of the women injured during their most recent physical assault, 30.2 percent said they received some type of medical treatment for their injury (exhibit 33). About three-quarters (76.1 percent) of the women who received medical treatment as a result of their most recent physical assault were treated in a hospital, either on an outpatient or inpatient basis. Among these women, 61.4 percent were treated in a hospital emergency department, 22.3 percent received other outpatient services, and 15.1 percent were treated on an inpatient basis. More than half (52.8 percent) of the medically treated female physical assault victims received treatment from a physician outside of a hospital setting, while 17.5 percent received ambulance or paramedic care, and less than one-tenth received dental care and/or physical therapy (exhibit 33).

Similar medical utilization patterns were found for male victims of physical assault: About one-third (37.1 percent) of the men injured during their most recent physical assault since age 18 received some type of medical treatment. Of these victims, 85.7 percent went to a hospital for treatment, while 42.1 percent saw a physician outside of a hospital setting. Of the male victims who went to a hospital for treatment, two-thirds (66.7 percent) were treated in an emergency department (exhibit 33).

Some victims received more than one type of medical treatment (e.g., hospitalization as well as outpatient physical therapy). Others received a type of medical treatment more than once—for example, 3 nights in the hospital or 10 physical therapy sessions. Hence, the annual number of medical treatments provided to rape and physical assault victims exceeds the annual number of rapes and physical assaults that resulted in treatment.

Exhibit 34 provides estimates of the average number of nights spent in the hospital and visits made to specific medical providers by rape and physical assault victims. These estimates are based on responses from victims who received the specific type of medical care considered. For example, the estimate of the average number of nights spent in the hospital by female rape victims (3.6) is based only on responses by female rape victims treated in a hospital on an inpatient basis. Note that some of these average frequency estimates have a relatively high margin of error (see footnotes c through f in exhibit 34) and should be viewed with caution.

Annual Health Care Utilization Estimates for Rape and Physical Assault Victims

Exhibit 35 presents estimates of the number of female rapes and female and male physical assaults resulting in injuries annually and estimates of the number of specific types of medical treatment these victimizations receive annually. The estimates presented in exhibit 35 were derived by applying the injury and health care utilization estimates presented in exhibits 30, 33, and 34 to annual victimization estimates presented in exhibit 5 (see chapter 3, "Prevalence and Incidence of Rape, Physical Assault,

and Stalking"). Because annual rape victimization estimates are based on responses from only 24 women who reported having been raped, they should be viewed with caution.

According to estimates generated by the NVAW Survey, hospital emergency department personnel treated approximately 1.26 million rape and physical assault injury victimizations in the 12 months preceding the survey (128,736 female rape victimizations, 546,902 female physical assault victimizations, and 588,256 male physical assault victimizations). This figure is somewhat lower than an estimate generated

| | Estimated Number of Victimizations per Year | | |
| | Rape Victims[a] | Physical Assault Victims | |
	Women	Women	Men
Victimization	876,064[b]	5,931,053	7,883,580
Victimization resulting in injury	275,960[b]	2,313,111	1,970,895
Victimization resulting in medical care	98,242[b]	693,933	729,231
Victimization resulting in:			
Hospital care	80,460[b]	527,389	627,139
Physician care	53,837[b]	367,784	306,277
Dental care	16,603[b]	69,393	80,215
Ambulance/paramedic care	18,666[b]	124,908	175,015
Physical therapy	16,406[b]	62,454	94,800
Victimization resulting in hospital care:			
Emergency room visit	40,230[b]	321,707	420,183
Outpatient visit	29,609[b]	116,026	144,242
Overnight in hospital	10,621[b]	79,108	62,714
Total number of:			
Emergency room visits	128,736[b]	546,902	588,256
Outpatient visits	65,140[b]	580,130[b]	403,878
Overnights in hospital	144,828[b]	672,418[b]	834,096
Physician visits	258,418[b]	1,213,687	2,205,194
Dental visits	83,015[b]	263,694	457,226
Ambulance/paramedic care	22,399[b]	137,399	175,015
Physical therapy visits	213,278[b]	1,155,399[b]	1,023,840

Exhibit 35. Average Annual Injury and Medical Utilization Estimates for Adult Rape and Physical Assault Victims by Victim Gender

[a]The number of male rape victims was insufficient to reliably calculate medical utilization estimates.
[b]Relative standard error exceeds 30 percent.

from the Study of Injured Victims of Violence (SIVV), a hospital record-extraction study conducted for the Bureau of Justice Statistics by the U.S. Consumer Product Safety Commission. The SIVV found that during 1994 hospital emergency department personnel treated an estimated 1.4 million people for injuries from confirmed or *suspected* interpersonal violence.[2] Included in the SIVV estimate (but excluded from the NVAW Survey estimate) are hospital emergency department treatments to victims of all ages (including children and adolescents), victims of *suspected* interpersonal violence, male rape victims, and male and female sexual assault and robbery victims. Because these groups were excluded from the NVAW Survey estimate, it is not surprising that it is lower than the SIVV estimate. The estimates from the NVAW Survey and the SIVV are quite similar, given that the two studies used very different research methods (i.e., victimization survey versus a medical record extraction study).

Rates of Violence-Related Injury and Accidental Injury

To place the injury and medical utilization estimates generated by the NVAW Survey in context, researchers compared the average annual injury victimization rate for women and men in the United States generated by the survey with the average annual rate of accidental injuries at work and the average annual rate of motor vehicle crash injuries for women and men in the United States. The combined average annual rate of rape and physical assault injury for women and men in the United States is 24 injury victimizations per 1,000 persons age 18 and older. This figure is derived by adding the estimated number of female rape victimizations and female and male physical assault victimizations that resulted in the victim being injured in the year preceding the survey, dividing this figure by the estimated number of women and men in the country who were age 18 and older at the time of the survey, and setting this figure to a population base of 1,000 [275,960 + 2,313,111 + 1,970,895 = 4,559,966 ÷ 193,445,000 = 0.0236 x 1,000 = 23.6].

In comparison the average annual rate of injury for a motor vehicle crash is 22 per 1,000 U.S. adults, and the average annual rate of accidental injury at work is 47 per 1,000 U.S. adults.[3] Thus women and men in the United States are nearly equally likely to be injured during an automobile crash as during a rape or physical assault; however, they are nearly twice as likely to be injured on the job than during a rape or physical assault.

Notes

1. For a more detailed discussion of injuries associated with rapes and physical assaults perpetrated against women and men by intimate partners, see Tjaden, P., and N. Thoennes, *Extent, Nature, and Consequences of Intimate Partner Violence: Findings From the National Violence Against Women Survey*, Research Report, Washington, DC: U.S. Department of Justice, National Institute of Justice, 2000, NCJ 181867.

2. Rand, M., *Violence-Related Injuries Treated in Hospital Emergency Departments*, Special Report, Washington, DC: U.S. Department of Justice, Bureau of Justice Statistics, 1997, NCJ 156921.

3. Bureau of Justice Statistics, "Highlights From 20 Years of Surveying Crime Victims," Special Report, Washington, DC: U.S. Department of Justice, Bureau of Justice Statistics, 1993, NCJ 144525.

9. Policy Implications

The NVAW Survey provides comprehensive data on the prevalence, incidence, and consequences of violence against women and victims' utilization of medical services. Information presented in this report can help inform policy and intervention directed at violence against women. Based on findings from the NVAW Survey, the authors conclude the following:

1. Violence against women should be treated as a significant social problem. The survey findings validate opinions held by many professionals about the pervasiveness of violence against women. More than half of the surveyed women reported being physically assaulted by an adult caretaker as a child and/or as an adult by another adult, and nearly one-fifth reported being raped at some time in their lives. Further, 2.1 percent of the surveyed women reported being raped, physically assaulted, or both in the previous 12 months. This equates to an estimated 2.1 million U.S. women who are raped and/or physically assaulted annually. Because some rape and physical assault victims experience multiple victimizations per year, an estimated 876,000 rapes and 5.9 million physical assaults, or 6.8 million rapes and physical assaults combined, are committed against U.S. women annually. (Because annual rape victimization estimates are based on responses from only 24 women who reported having been raped, they should be viewed with caution.) Given the pervasiveness of rape and physical assault among American women, violence against women should be treated as a major criminal justice and public health concern.

2. Rape should be viewed as a crime committed against youths as well as adults. The survey confirms previous reports that most rape victims are victimized before age 18. One of 6 surveyed women (17.6 percent) reported they had experienced an attempted or completed forcible rape at some time in their life. Of these, 21.6 percent were less than age 12 when they were first raped, while 32.4 percent were ages 12 to 17. Thus, more than one-half (54 percent) of the female rape victims identified by the survey were raped before age 18. The survey also found that women who reported being raped before age 18 were significantly more likely to report being raped as adults. Given these findings, rape prevention strategies should focus on rapes committed against minors as well as adults, and rape research should focus on the long-term effects of rape occurring at an early age.

3. Physical assault of children by adult caretakers is widespread. Using a definition of physical assault that includes a range of behaviors from slapping and hitting to using a gun, the survey found that 40.0 percent of surveyed women and 53.8 percent of surveyed men reported being physically assaulted by a parent, stepparent, or other adult caretaker as a child. Because questions about physical assault experienced as a child at the hands of an adult caretaker were framed in terms of violence committed by adult caretakers, it can be assumed that respondents who disclosed this type of assault defined these acts as violence at the time of the interview. The survey also found that women and men who reported they were physically assaulted by an adult caretaker as a child were twice as likely to report being physically assaulted as an adult. Given these findings, future research should focus on the link between physical assault in childhood and physical assault in adulthood.

4. Stalking is more widespread than previously thought. Although it uses a definition of stalking that requires victims to feel a high level of fear, the survey found stalking is more wide-spread than previously thought: 8.1 percent of surveyed women and 2.2 percent of surveyed men reported being stalked at some time in their life, and 1.0 percent of surveyed women and 0.4 percent of surveyed men reported being stalked in the previous 12 months. Thus, an estimated 1.4 million women and men are stalked annually in the United States. These estimates are greater than previous nonscientific "guesstimates" of stalking prevalence. Moreover, if a less stringent definition of stalking is used—one requiring victims to feel somewhat frightened or a little frightened of their assailant's behavior—the lifetime stalking prevalence rate increases dramatically, from 8 to 12 percent for women and 2 to 4 percent for men; annual stalking prevalence rates increase from 1 to 6 percent for women and 0.4 to 1.5 percent for men. Given the large number of stalking victims, it is important that stalking be treated as a legitimate criminal justice problem and public health concern.

5. Studies are needed to determine why the prevalence of rape, physical assault, and stalking varies significantly among women and men of different racial and ethnic backgrounds. The survey found that American Indian/Alaska Native women reported significantly more rape and stalking victimization than white women or African-American women and that mixed-race women reported significantly more rape victimization than white women. The survey also found that Hispanic women reported significantly less rape victimization than non-Hispanic women. Finally, the survey found that American Indian/Alaska Native men reported significantly more physical assault victimization than did Asian men.

It is unclear from the survey data whether differences in prevalence rates among women and men of different racial groups and between Hispanic and non-Hispanic women are caused by differences in reporting practices or differences in actual victimization experiences. It is also unclear how social, environmental, and demographic factors intersect with race and ethnicity to produce differences in rape, physical assault,

and stalking prevalence among women and men of different racial and ethnic backgrounds. More research is needed to establish the degree of variance in prevalence among women and men of different racial and ethnic groups and to determine how much of the variance may be explained by differences in willingness to disclose information to interviewers and how much by social, environmental, and demographic factors. Research is also needed to determine whether differences exist in rape, physical assault, and stalking prevalence among women and men of diverse Asian/Pacific Islander groups, American Indian tribes, and Alaska Native communities.

6. Women are at greater risk of intimate partner violence than men. The survey found that women were significantly more likely than men to report being raped, physically assaulted, and/or stalked by a current or former intimate partner, whether the timeframe considered was the person's lifetime or the previous 12 months. Specifically, 24.8 percent of surveyed women and 7.6 percent of surveyed men said they were raped and/or physically assaulted by a current or former spouse, cohabiting partner, boyfriend/girlfriend, or date in their lifetime, while 1.5 percent of surveyed women and 0.9 percent of surveyed men were raped and/or physically assaulted by such an assailant in the previous 12 months. In addition, 4.8 percent of surveyed women, compared with 0.6 percent of surveyed men, reported being stalked by an intimate partner in their lifetime, while 0.5 percent of surveyed women and 0.2 percent of surveyed men were stalked by an intimate partner in the previous 12 months. Moreover, women who were raped or physically assaulted by a current or former intimate partner were significantly more likely to sustain injuries than men who were raped or physically assaulted by a current or former intimate partner. Given these findings, intimate partner violence should be considered first and foremost a crime against women.

7. Violence against women is predominantly intimate partner violence. Data from the survey confirm previous reports that violence against women is predominantly intimate partner violence. Of the women who reported being raped and/or physically assaulted since age 18, three-quarters (76 percent) were victimized by a current or former husband, cohabiting partner, boyfriend, or date. Of the women who were stalked since age 18, more than half (59.5 percent) were victimized by such a perpetrator. Given these findings, violence against women intervention strategies should focus on risks posed to women by current and former husbands, cohabiting partners, boyfriends, and dates.

8. America's medical community should receive comprehensive training about the medical needs of female victims of rape and physical assault. The injury and medical utilization data generated by the NVAW Survey provide compelling evidence of the physical and social costs associated with violence against women. The survey found that in about one-third of the rapes and physical assaults perpetrated against women, the victim sustains an injury.

Further, in about one-third of such injury victimizations, the victim receives some type of medical care (e.g., paramedic care, emergency room treatment, dental care, or physical therapy). Thus, of the estimated 6.8 million rapes and physical assaults committed against U.S. women annually, an estimated 1.5 million will result in the victim receiving some type of medical care. (As noted earlier, annual rape victimization estimates are based on responses from only 24 women and should therefore be viewed with caution.) Because many rape and physical assault victims receive multiple treatments for the same injury victimization, medical personnel in the United States treat literally millions of rape and physical assault victimizations annually.

Given the high number of injury victimizations perpetrated against women annually and the extensive nature of medical treatment to female victims of violence, medical professionals should receive information about the physical consequences of violence against women and the medical needs of female victims.

About the National Institute of Justice

The National Institute of Justice (NIJ), a component of the Office of Justice Programs, is the research agency of the U.S. Department of Justice. Created by the Omnibus Crime Control and Safe Streets Act of 1968, as amended, NIJ is authorized to support research, evaluation, and demonstration programs, development of technology, and both national and international information dissemination. Specific mandates of the Act direct NIJ to:

- Sponsor special projects and research and development programs that will improve and strengthen the criminal justice system and reduce or prevent crime.

- Conduct national demonstration projects that employ innovative or promising approaches for improving criminal justice.

- Develop new technologies to fight crime and improve criminal justice.

- Evaluate the effectiveness of criminal justice programs and identify programs that promise to be successful if continued or repeated.

- Recommend actions that can be taken by Federal, State, and local governments as well as by private organizations to improve criminal justice.

- Carry out research on criminal behavior.

- Develop new methods of crime prevention and reduction of crime and delinquency.

In recent years, NIJ has greatly expanded its initiatives, the result of the Violent Crime Control and Law Enforcement Act of 1994 (the Crime Act), partnerships with other Federal agencies and private foundations, advances in technology, and a new international focus. Examples of these new initiatives include:

- Exploring key issues in community policing, violence against women, violence within the family, sentencing reforms, and specialized courts such as drug courts.

- Developing dual-use technologies to support national defense and local law enforcement needs.

- Establishing four regional National Law Enforcement and Corrections Technology Centers and a Border Research and Technology Center.

- Strengthening NIJ's links with the international community through participation in the United Nations network of criminological institutes, the U.N. Criminal Justice Information Network, UNOJUST (United Nations Online Justice Clearinghouse), and the NIJ International Center.

- Improving the online capability of NIJ's criminal justice information clearinghouse.

- Establishing the ADAM (Arrestee Drug Abuse Monitoring) program—formerly the Drug Use Forecasting (DUF) program—to increase the number of drug-testing sites and study drug-related crime.

The Institute Director establishes the Institute's objectives, guided by the priorities of the Office of Justice Programs, the Department of Justice, and the needs of the criminal justice field. The Institute actively solicits the views of criminal justice professionals and researchers in the continuing search for answers that inform public policymaking in crime and justice.

To find out more about the National Institute of Justice,
please contact:

National Criminal Justice Reference Service
P.O. Box 6000
Rockville, MD 20849–6000
800–851–3420
e-mail: *askncjrs@ncjrs.org*

To obtain an electronic version of this document, access the NIJ Web site
(http://www.ojp.usdoj.gov/nij).

If you have questions, call or e-mail NCJRS.